it

ALEXA
CHUNG

PENGUIN BOOKS

Published by the Penguin Group
Penguin Group (USA) LLC
375 Hudson Street
New York, New York 10014

USA | Canada | UK | Ireland | Australia | New Zealand | India | South Africa | China
penguin.com
A Penguin Random House Company

First published in Great Britain by Particular Books 2013
Published in Penguin Books (USA) 2013
This edition published 2014

PICTURE CREDITS
pp. 26, 40, 41, 60, 63, 118 © Rex Features; pp. 55 (cat), 55 (Ronnie
Spector), 120 © Getty Images; pp. 114, 142 © Corbis; pp. 37, 39, 45
from the BFI National Archive;
p. 10 © Polygram/Alex Bailey; p. 29 © Regency/James Bridges;
p. 30 © MGM; p. 33 © Loren Shane Humphrey;
p. 34 © Touchstone/James Hamilton; p. 35 © Vogue;
p. 36 © Estate of Jeanloup Sieff; p. 42 © Heritage Images;
p. 43 © Juergen Teller; p. 46 © Tennessee Thomas; p. 61
Time & Life/Getty Images; p. 62 © ARGOS; p. 92 © Estate of
Sam Haskins, 2013; p. 107 (bottom) © Tennessee Thomas; p. 110 ©
William Coupon/Corbis; p. 112 © David Bailey/Camera Eye; p. 158 ©
David Titlow; p. 160 © Mark Hunter; p. 163 © Guy Aroch; p. 180 ©
Alan Davidson; p. 183 © Splash News

All other images © Alexa Chung

ISBN 978-0-14-312676-8

Printed in Italy by Graphicom srl
Colour reproduction by Altaimage
3 5 7 9 10 8 6 4 2

Designed by Stefanie Posavec

for Gill and Phil

A special thank you to my family and friends for offering me endless support and encouragement.

And to Helen – confidante, cheerleader and whip-cracker extraordinaire.

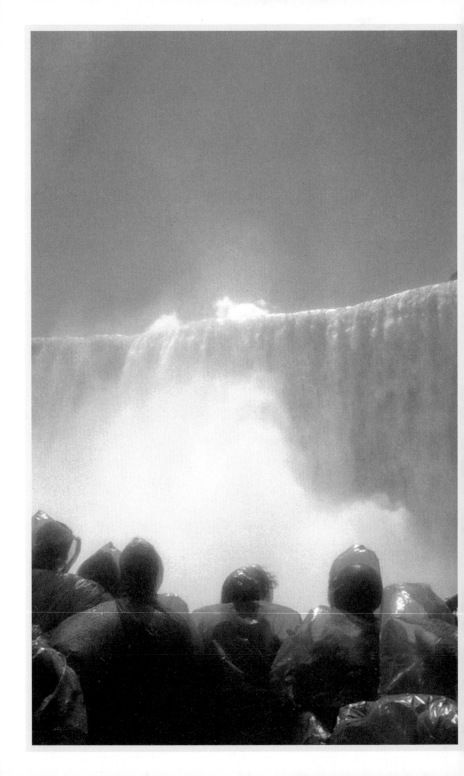

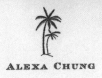

ALEXA CHUNG

it

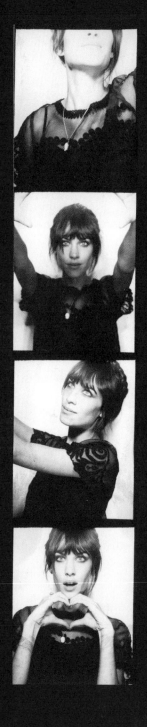

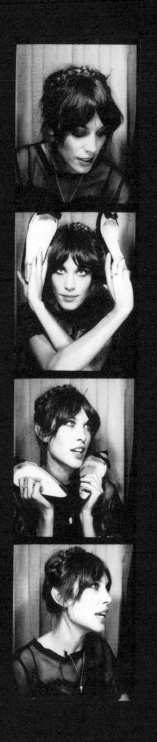

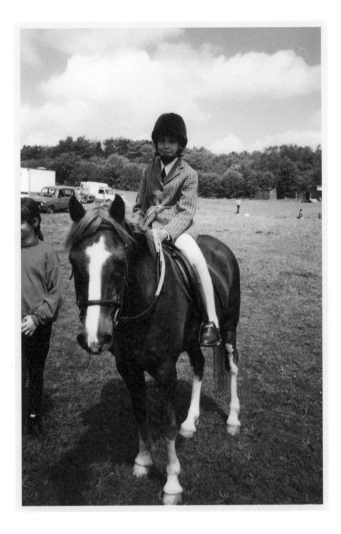

HORSES were my first love. I grew up in a village with more horses than people so this was a convenient passion but one that my parents didn't share. For my sixth birthday I got a riding lesson and was decked out in jodhpurs, a reversible sweatshirt and some new black boots. I begged my parents for seven years to let me have a pony. Obviously for the first few months they thought it was a fad that would pass but in the end it was a toss up between relenting and letting me have one or listening to me chant 'PLEASE PLEASE PLEASE CAN I HAVE A PONY', day in, day out for eternity. My first and last pony was called Pip. She was ploddy, difficult to jump and very lovely to draw. Looking back on it now, I think I was interested in ponies and all the relevant paraphernalia because of the fashion as much as the animals. That silhouette of skinny trousers, ankle boots and an oversized sweatshirt is one I never managed to get away from.

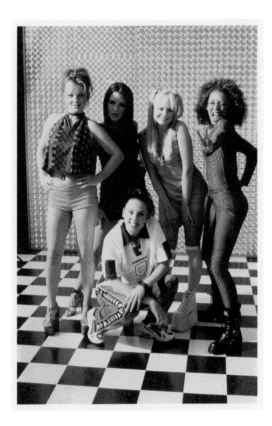

THE opening bars to 'Wannabe' were a call to arms. I was on a beach in Majorca when I first heard Mel B utter the still-confusing lyric 'Zigazigahhh!!!!' Little did I know (pre-internet and mobile phone) that my excited response to the Spice Girls hitting the scene was happening simultaneously to just about every tweenage girl with access to a radio. The Spice Girls appeared out of nowhere like a tidal wave of positive energy that smashed anything and everything in their way. Upon discovering what they looked like, I was smitten. Five young(ish) women, in bright colours, each with their own identity, screaming 'GIRL POWER!' at the top of their lungs. This was the band I'd been waiting for. Sure, they threw a spanner in the works of my rapidly evolving taste in music, but that's fine because what I missed in musical education I more than made up for in a newfound passion for glittery eyeshadow, crop tops I filled with tissue, and impossible-to-walk-in platform trainers. At a time when I was morphing from awkward child to awkward teenager, the Spice Girls supported me like the training bra of womanhood.

As far as fashion influence goes the Spice Girls must be held accountable for all the poor sartorial decisions I made between the years 1996–8. Their version of sixties fashion in the nineties was affordable and alluring but somehow got mangled through my reinterpretation. Union Jack dress? Check. Buffalo boots? Yep. Pigtails? Uh-huh. Leopard print everything? Sure. I made the mistake of attempting to emulate the style of the entire band simultaneously. But at least they got it right (in a tacky, crass, colourful way). The video for 'Stop' is my particular favourite – Geri is sporting a beehive, blue rollneck and kilt whilst riding a donkey through a village. Genius. My mother let me dye my hair like Ginger Spice because I thought she was The Most Beautiful Woman I had ever seen and, let's be honest, I probably first heard about Gucci via Posh Spice. To this day I like to work a Posh-esque point and pout into my arsenal of dance moves. I dance like a moving catalogue, so it fits in perfectly.

Sometimes it saddens me to think I was introduced to the concept of feminism by a manufactured pop group masterminded by opportunistic men, but hey ho, you gotta start somewhere. The Spice Girls' brand of Girl Power made me appreciate my mother ('Mama I Love You'), girlfriends ('If you wanna be my lover, you gotta get with my friends … ') and (although I didn't know it at the time) they were promoting safe sex in '2 Become 1' – an unusual subject matter to broach in a song.

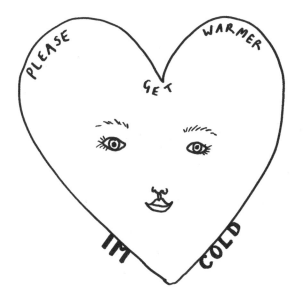

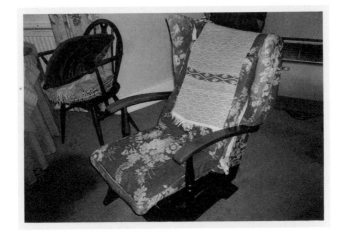

MY Grandpa Kwan was a skinny Chinese man who used to pinch me quite a lot to show me how much he liked me. We bonded on Sundays because the only part of an English roast either of us would eat were the potatoes and Yorkshire puddings. I respected his taste in food almost as much as his taste in clothes. During the eighties my mum and dad would buy him shirts for Christmas that he would politely unwrap (very, very slowly), place beside him and proceed to never, ever wear. It wasn't until I got older that I realized Grandpa Kwan had serious style. On a typical day he would wear his thick tortoise-shell glasses, a stripy shirt, a navy tank top, brown skinny cords, a navy flat cap and whatever the latest Nike trainers were. In fact, Grandpa Kwan was a fashion legend.

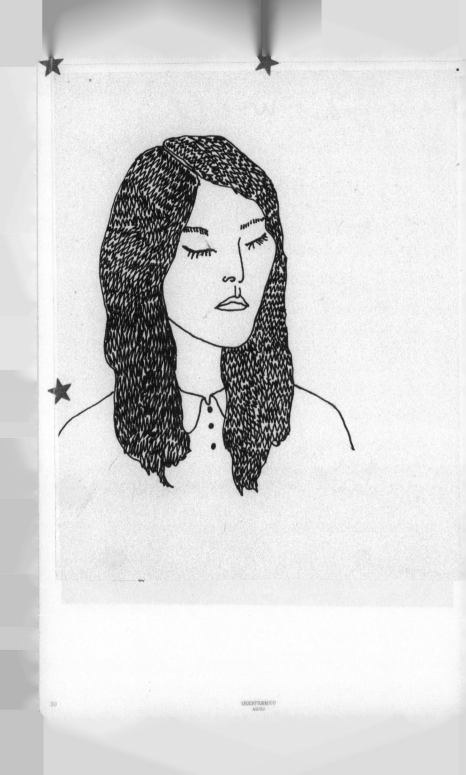

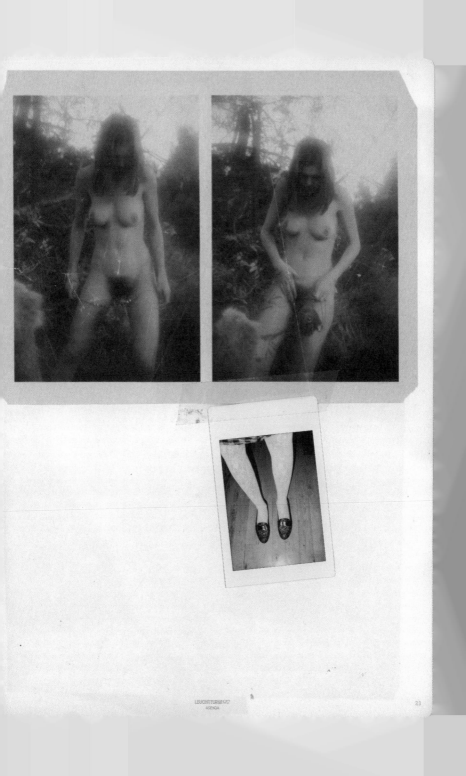

W H E N I was thirteen I spent a lot of time pretending to like dance music because everyone at my school seemed to love it. If only I'd known it was OK to have different tastes to others and that one day my mind would be blown open by an older man who would introduce me to The Smiths, The Cure, Buzzcocks, Talking Heads and almost every other band I adore to this day. I also wish I'd been reassured that one day, yes, a boy would actually fancy me in spite and potentially, deliberately, FOR my zero boob/skinny legs combo. But mainly I wish I'd listened to my mother when she said learning to play the piano might come in handy in the future and would actually be something I would thank her for forcing me to do. Every Wednesday we would drive to Mrs Batten's house listening to *The Archers*, with me in the passenger seat trying desperately to think up excuses for why I hadn't practiced that week. Though it seemed very unlikely at the time, I am thankful for those piano lessons every time I manage to impress a boy by hammering out some Chopin when drunk (swot up, kids!).

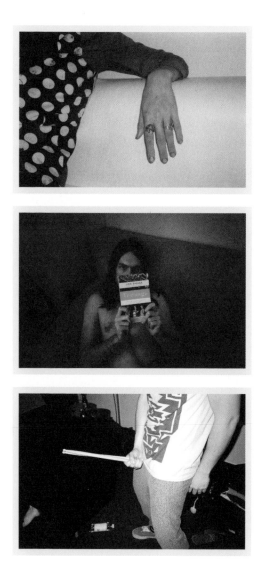

I met my best friend Misty Fox at a casting for a music video. We had to pretend to be best friends in the audition and were so convincing that we were given the job and have continued to be best pals ever since. Misty knows pretty much every secret I have ever kept and even some I've forgotten.

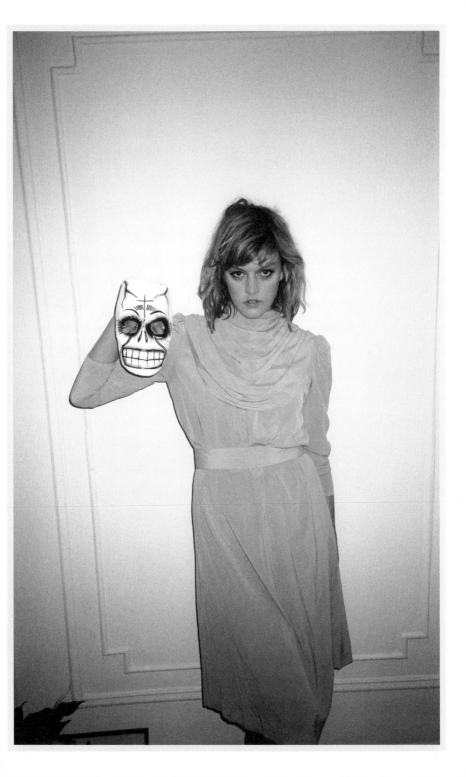

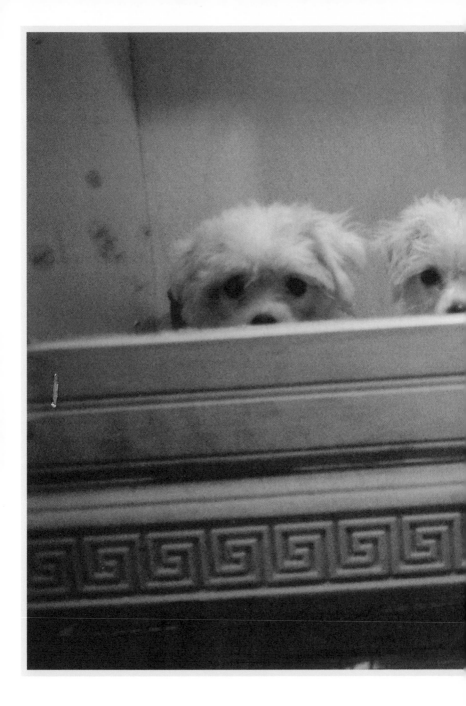

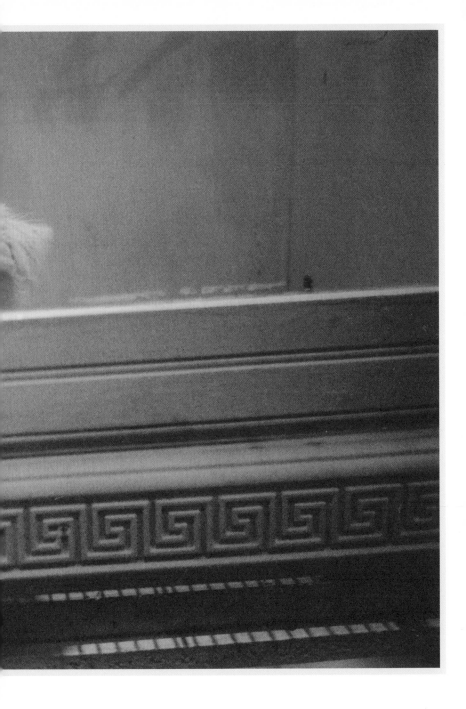

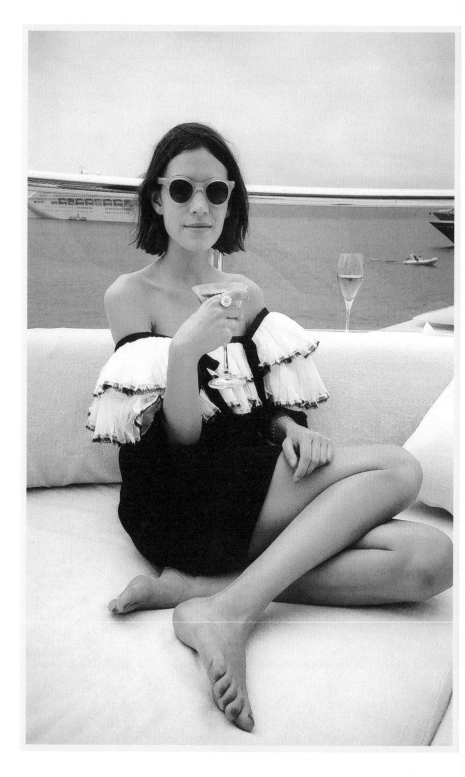

WHILE I was figuring out my own personal style I borrowed heavily from the stars of the silver screen. I still find film characters to be the most useful sources of inspiration when it comes to sartorial decisions, but now rather than literally ripping off a look and seeming as though I'm in fancy dress as a particular character, I manage to incorporate certain styles into my wardrobe in a more subtle way. Apart from when I'm trying to be Wednesday Addams, because that look is DEAD ON.

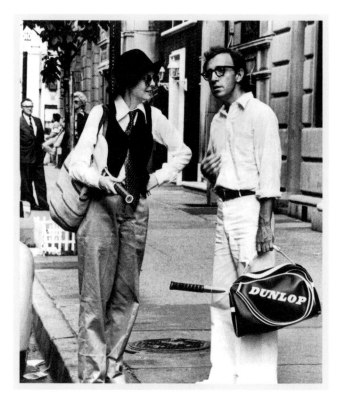

T H E first film character I truly fell in love with because of the way she dressed was Annie Hall. It was the first Woody Allen film I'd ever seen and it sent me into a three-year obsession with just about anything he had made, regardless of the quality. I responded to Hall's scatty, ditzy personality and the way it was at odds with her very masculine way of dressing. Her character seemed so realistic and complete, and in part that's because of the stylish wardrobe. Nobody ever made high-waisted trousers and a tie look as good as Annie Hall. Her femininity, mixed with tomboyish silhouettes and scruffy thrown-together looks, is something I still reference heavily now. I love the seventies dork glasses, the striped men's shirts, the great tweed jackets and frilly Victorian tops she mixes together so well. It was the first time I recognized that sexuality didn't have to be expressed through thigh-high skirts and tight tops. As a teenager, this was somewhat of a revelation. Although Hall may be one of the most neurotic characters to grace a screen, her clothes suggest a laid back elegance that I strive to achieve when getting dressed.

AT the other end of the sexy scale we have Liv Tyler in *Empire Records* and her overtly provocative get-up as the teen fantasy vixen. Her schoolgirl kilt with cropped mohair jumper and heavy man boots just looks perfect. I love the proportions, I love how it is childish but also deliberately alluring. It suggests a sense of humour, an ironic take on schoolgirl stripper outfits. It's a really really cool version of the Britney Spears ' ... Baby One More Time' video costume. If Tyler had a scrap of make-up on with this look it would push it into the obscene, but worn with a fresh face it does the job perfectly. A generation of young men swooned and I awkwardly tried to replicate this look at sixth form. It didn't have the desired effect.

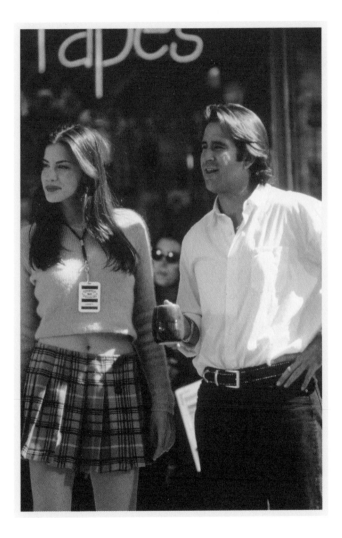

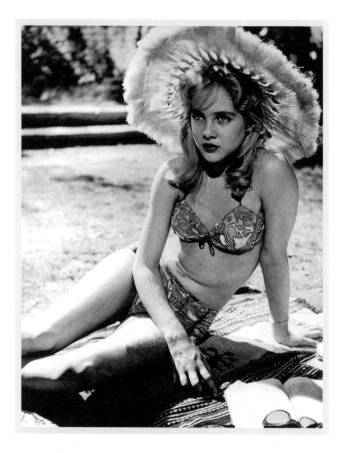

LOLITA is my favourite book. She's also my favourite character to reference when getting dressed in summer months. Obviously, this look is age dependent, but until people start throwing rotten tomatoes at me in the street it's an inspiration I'm willing to plunder. I love her heart-shaped glasses. Heart. Shaped. Glasses. So cool. Also the hotpants and cropped blouse combo. The matchy-matchy bikini with high-waisted shorts. Pigtails. It can look ridiculous if you're under sixteen or over twenty-five but I'm willing to keep paying tribute to this limby literary icon ... at least for the time being.

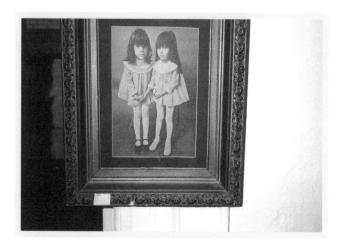

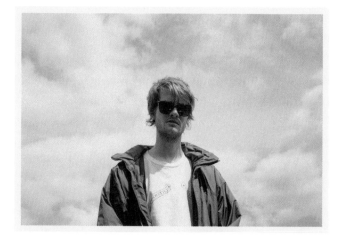

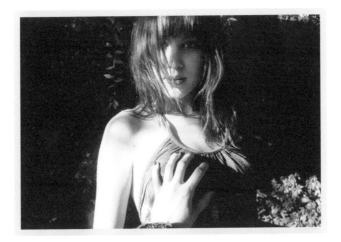

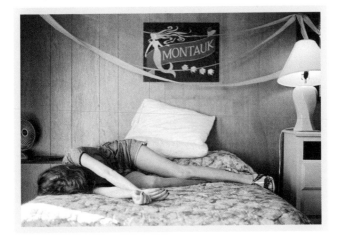

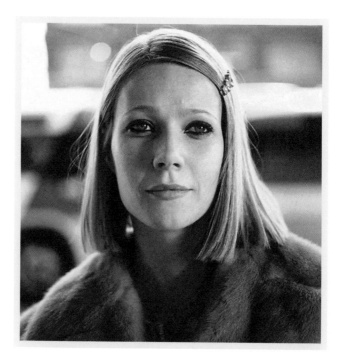

MARGOT Tenenbaum's kohl-eyed, chain-smoking appearance in *The Royal Tenenbaums*: I love her side-parted bob and preppy Lacoste dresses. The fur coat over a tennis dress. In America I see a thousand Margot tributes on Halloween but that's because she's so damn cool and the look is timeless.

CIAO Manhattan – What can I say? Edie Bloody Sedgwick. How much make-up can one person pile on their face? How many drugs can one girl do? A lot, is the answer. Sedgwick at her finest, in black tights, cropped hair (an ode to Warhol) and swinging leopard jacket. The earrings, the mini mini mini dresses. Sedgwick's poor little rich girl persona and wardrobe never gets old even when it gets older. Having said that, my favourite image has to be this one, from US *Vogue*, 1966.

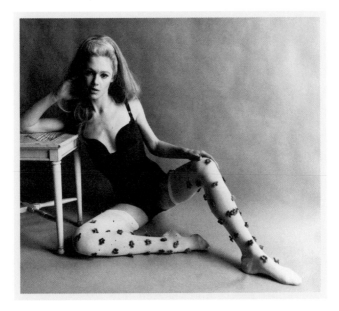

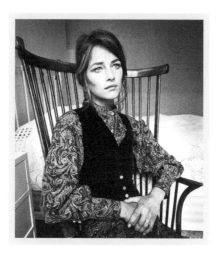

THE Night Porter is insane, but thanks to Charlotte Rampling, who has quite possibly the best face of all time, the costumes look incredible. Obviously people have referenced the SS uniform of trousers, braces, and a patent leather cap that Rampling wears in one iconic scene time and time again, but my main interest is in the prissy-prim outfits she has on in the rest of the film. I love the pastel colours, the hair bands, the Mary Janes. So wrong it's right.

Rampling's personal style is also hugely inspiring. Her face matches her clothes in that both are incredibly pretty and yet somehow masculine.

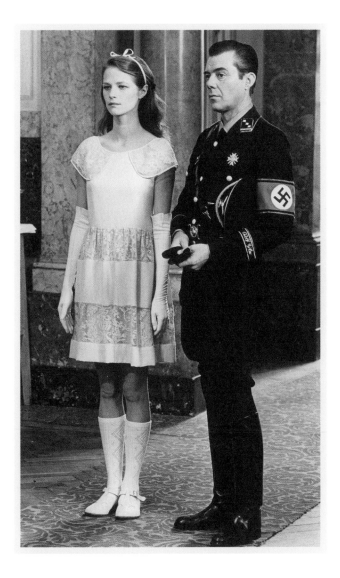

LADIES and Gentlemen, the Fabulous Stains is brilliant ... if you like an angry girl punk precursor to riot grrrl, which thankfully I do. Check out the make-up, the hair, the clothes. If you want to rebel and show that no, you won't do what your boss/mother/friends say, this is perfect wardrobe inspiration for you. WARNING: One look doesn't suit all. Prepare to shout.

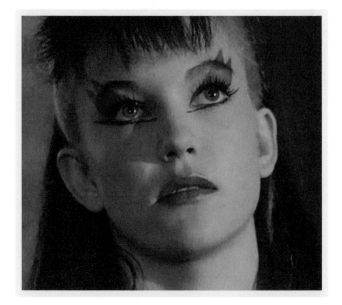

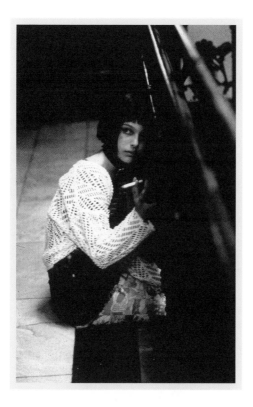

NATALIE Portman in *Léon* made a lot of grown men feel very uncomfortable. I completely understand. In the same vein as Lolita but with a badass edge, Mathilda's tomboyish style was a stroke of genius. I love her choker, I love her bomber jacket, but most of all I love her attitude.

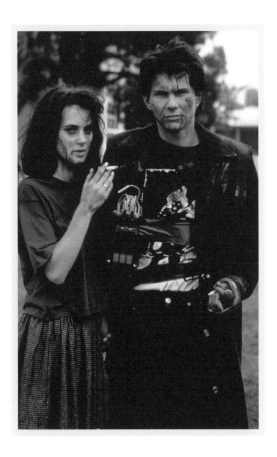

WINONA Ryder in the film *Heathers* is about as badass as it gets. Her clothes reflect her good-girl-gone-bad character (way before Rihanna tried it). The preppy waspy penny loafer and kilt combo is killer, Heather.

WEDNESDAY Addams was probably the first film character I saw to wear the Peter Pan collar. Match that with pigtails and gothy pale skin and she's pretty much my favourite style icon. Addams' inability to crack a smile neatly sets off the sombre outfit. Obsessed.

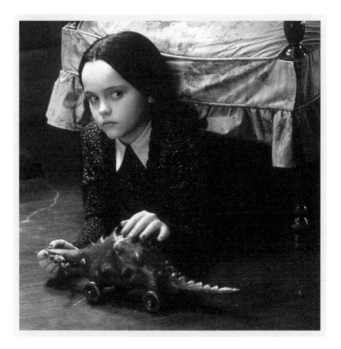

I'VE always been jealous of girls who can skateboard (like Jodie) and many times I've tried to master the art. From what I can tell, to be good at skateboarding you need to be fearless, coordinated and twelve. I am none of these things. Skateboarding to men is what hotpants are to women: it all looks very wrong once you reach a certain age. Nobody likes to be told it's over.

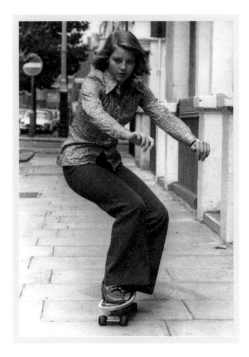

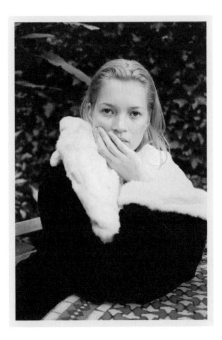

AT this point trillions of pictures have been taken of Kate Moss in an effort to capture her beauty, style and essence. Yet our appetite for more, more, more rages on unabated. She's paid very well to sell us things that we might previously have had no interest in buying. That's because anything she puts near her body is instantly transformed into the coolest thing ever, because *She* is the coolest thing ever and nobody can explain why. It's just a fact.

AND now to Anna Karina in *Une Femme Est une Femme*. The Dream. The sailor outfit she has on before stripping down to perfect lacy sixties underwear. The raincoat and red tights combo. The weird blue santa-ish outfit with the white fur trimming and matching blue hair bow. STOP BEING PERFECT, ANNA KARINA! I also love how she has one red cardigan that she either wears normally or turns backwards so it buttons up at the back. So French, so cute, so ... Whenever I watch this film I spend the whole time taking photos of the screen. I just want to be her (but without the crazy baby obsession).

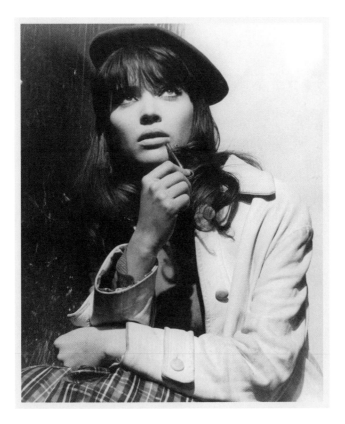

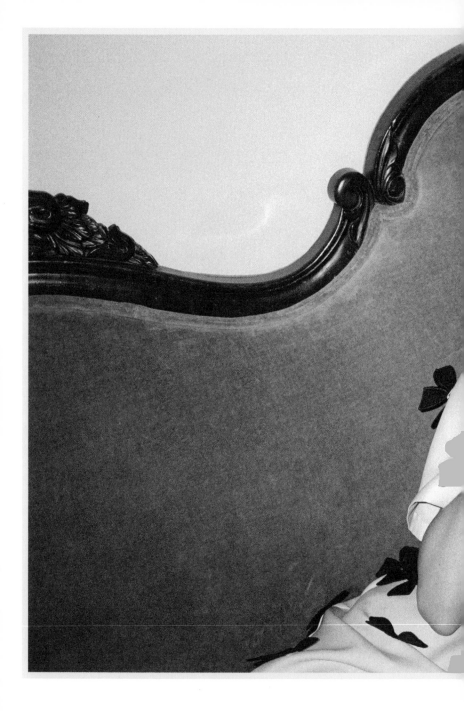

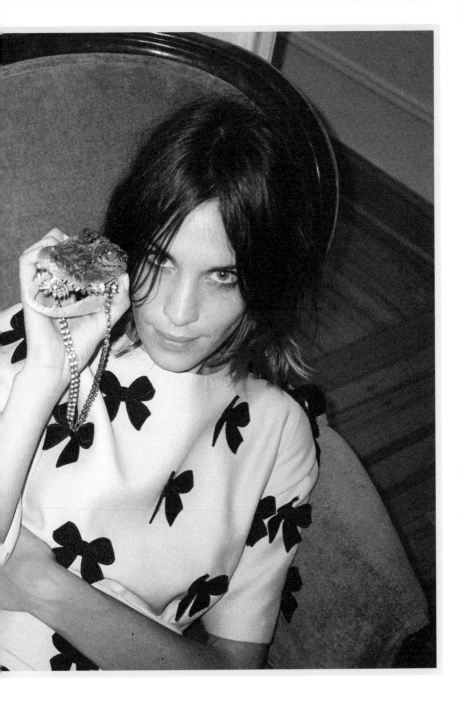

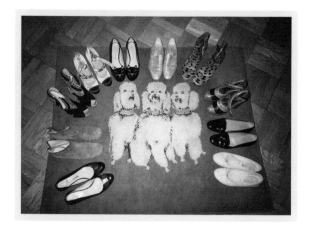

GETTING dressed in the morning can be difficult. My main problem is that I'm incredibly messy so my floor/bed/trunk/towel rail – really anything solid – becomes my wardrobe. It's like an oil spill if oil was clothes. Anyway, my point is I'm fairly certain a more organized person would be able to get dressed in the morning without a hitch because an organized person would probably pick their outfit the night before. This goes against everything I stand for – i.e., being spontaneous and impulsive. It is that same impulsive quality that has seen me purchase some incredibly foul items (see floor problem). Amidst the chaos I have, however, managed to formulate some kind of guide to getting dressed.

HERE IT IS:

1. In the shower/bath/over the sink (I don't know what you like) take your time to imagine your day and how you'd like to look as you are doing all those boring tasks/potentially running into an ex or future partner/nemesis ...

2. Is the outfit clean? – Is it though???

3. Try and find the things.

4. Put it on, and this is crucial ... *look in a mirror.*

5. Do the clothes fit properly? Is there a VPL problem? Will you be able to scale stairs without flashing someone? Is walking going to be a problem in those shoes? Do you look like a wizard or crazy person or someone who has done too many mushrooms? If so go back to stage 1.

You're welcome.

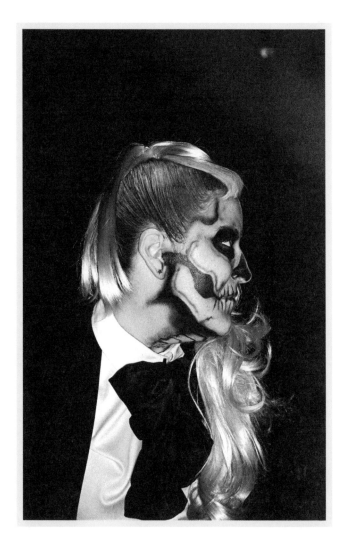

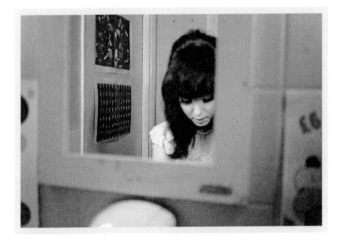

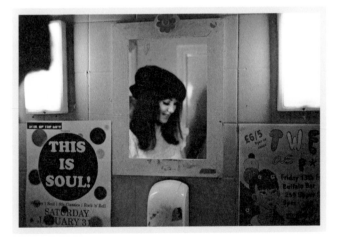

MY first interaction with make-up was, I imagine, a universal one. I used to watch my mother painting her nails and applying lipstick and mimic her as she was getting ready. By the age of eleven I had progressed to experimenting with silver eyeshadow and dark brown lipstick. I blame these colour choices on the nineties: watching endless episodes of *My So-Called Life* and obsessing over a space-themed Levi's advert. By the time I was a teenager I was struggling to understand the correct way to apply foundation and felt like I was supposed to wear it when I definitely didn't need to and probably looked like a pageant child (no photos of this era exist – presumably my parents had the foresight and compassion not to capture it on film). And then I started modelling at the age of sixteen and was subjected to all sorts of glittery, smoky, sticky, sexy, oily, unpolished experiments with my face.

Despite all of that playing around I still think make-up is a difficult thing to get right. In a perfect world we wouldn't need to wear it at all, but unless you want to deal with that make-up tattoo situation, that's not an option for most women. For me, if I don't want to look like Dave

Grohl past 11 a.m., it's sort of a must. Personally for a daytime look I like to keep things natural. Often for photoshoots or TV I have stronger make-up on so on days off I just tend to moisturise, add concealer, mascara, blusher and lip balm.

Some things I've learnt from being lucky enough to have my make-up done professionally: a little eyelash curl goes a long way, especially if, like me you have what could pass as a row of iron filings for eyelashes. With lip balm it's best to stick to Australian pawpaw cream or natural products to avoid a massive lip peel which can happen when you use glosses or overly fragranced products. Your mouth should always look kissable and to that end I will occasionally exfoliate my lips (sounds disgusting, sort of is). An impromptu exfoliation kit I have used in the past is some Vaseline and brown sugar, which I rub onto my mouth and rinse off with warm water. In the winter this can restore your wind-chapped lips to dewy summer status. With blusher it took me a while to perfect the art of application without going overboard and coming over all Aunt Sal. A dot of cream blush on each cheek blended with my fingertips is the approach I now take for that slightly flushed but not overly embarrassed look. I prefer cream blushers to powders because I'm weird and have this aversion to anything dry on my face. I am obsessed with moisturising. I am also obsessed with cigarettes – so I like to think the two balance each other out.

So that's a classic crawl-out-of-bed face overhaul, but if I know I'm going out for the day and potentially into the night I add a cat-eye eyeliner. I stole this look from Cleopatra and Ronnie Spector from The Ronettes and I think it's pretty much the most flattering make-up of all time. The two problems you'll encounter if you're trying to line the top of your lid are finding an eyeliner that doesn't smudge all over your face and being able to draw in a straight line. I cannot help you with either of these things other than to say practice makes perfect and always think 'up and out'. The thing you're trying to fake is making your eyes look wider and more cat-like. Now study a cat's face. Yeah, that.

Liquid liners in a pen form are best for control and staying power. I find the pot with the wand with the brush on the end of it was probably invented for the sole purpose of causing

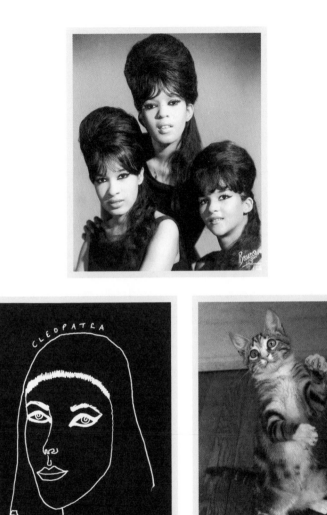

pre-leaving-the-house meltdowns. Someone evil designed it.

My addiction to cat-eye eyeliner started long before I knew who I was referencing. My first TV job meant that I had a professional make-up artist applying professional make-up to my unprofessional (hungover) face. We decided that all things considered we should play up my eyes as on TV eye contact is imperative. Once I had the black line traced on my top lid for the first time it was game over and no other make-up choices got a look in. It's sexy and classic without seeming too much. (Apparently Cleopatra may have lined her eyes with kohl liner not just to look rad but also to help ward off disease.)

Eyeliner aside, sometimes I go crazy and add a red lip to my make-up look, but it has to be a very special occasion. That's a lie actually, because one top tip I have is if I'm looking tired I wear a red lip to detract from my heavy eyebags. *WARNING* this can make you look as though you haven't been to bed but came to work straight from a very special occasion. Also, a red lip is great to wear in airports. I don't know why but it makes me feel very glamorous to have bothered to apply lipstick when I'm travelling. To pack for flying: red lipstick, moisturiser, concealer, hand sanitizer, a can of dry shampoo and a mirror, because queueing for the loo and managing to do a beauty overhaul before they turn the seatbelt sign on is nigh-on impossible.

Obviously different make-up suits different faces and it's best to work out which features you'd like to play up and then experiment (in the house). Also work out which things don't suit you, e.g.: I look odd when I'm overly tanned and so bronzer has never been my thing because I don't like anything false as I feel like I'm lying to myself. In winter when things start getting very pale I just go with it and try and get into a gothic mood. Eyeliner inside my eye makes me look like I'm giving people evils so I try to avoid that, whereas it really looks brilliant on my friend Lizzy, who has rounder eyes than me.

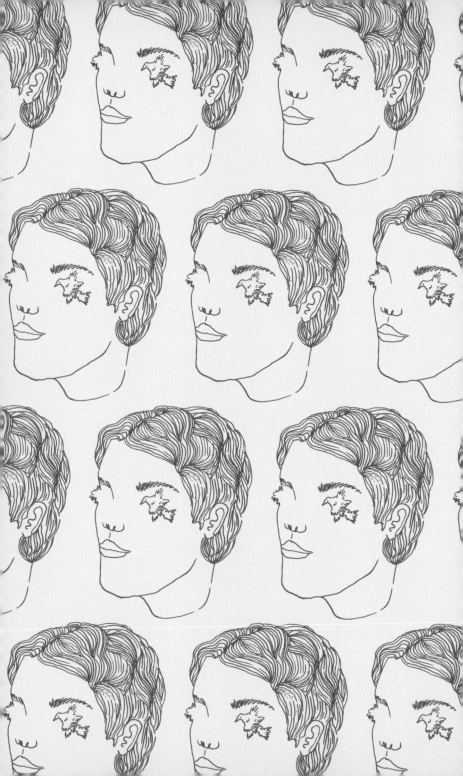

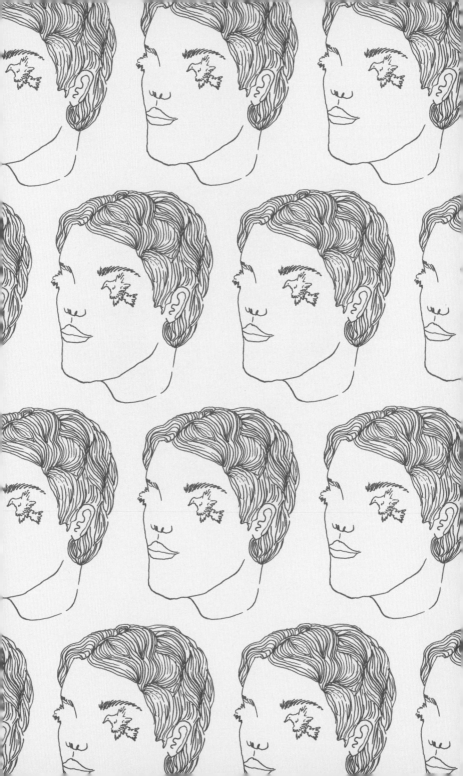

HERE ARE SOME BEAUTY
LOOKS I LOVE:

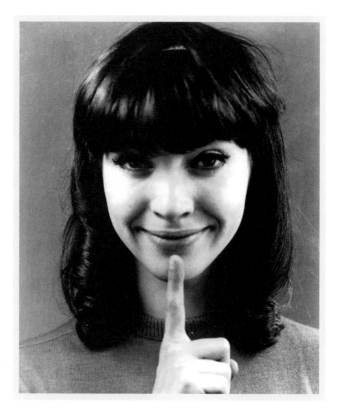

*If eyeliner is your thing, Anna
Karina owns that look.*

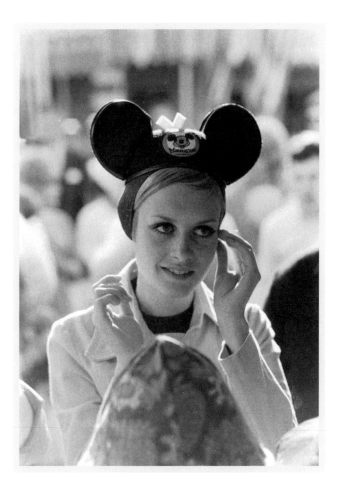

*Twiggy is perfect. Pile mascara
onto your bottom lashes to play up
saucer eyes. Mouse ears optional.*

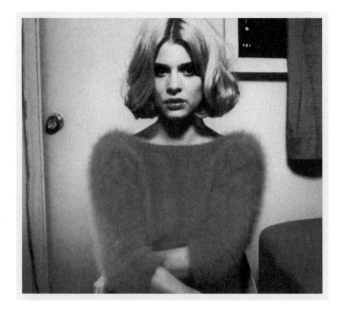

Or how about a hot pink lip like Nastassja
Kinski in Paris, Texas?

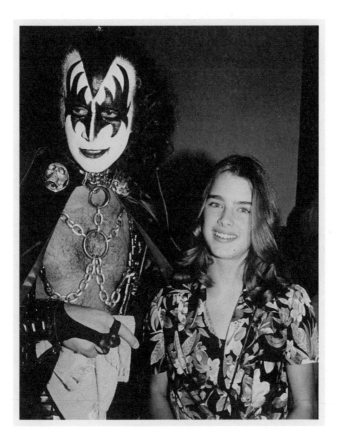

Long before 'scouse brows', there was
Brooke Shields.

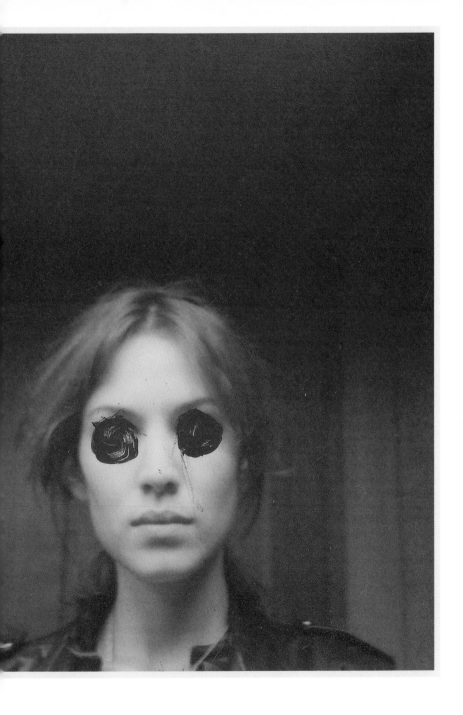

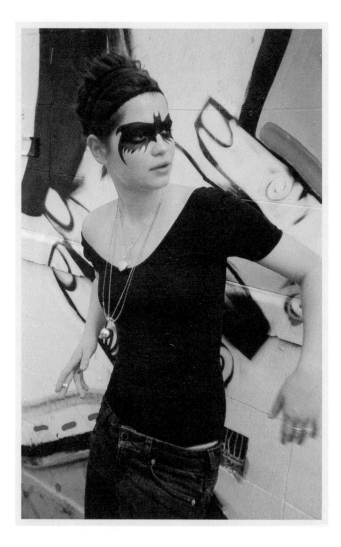

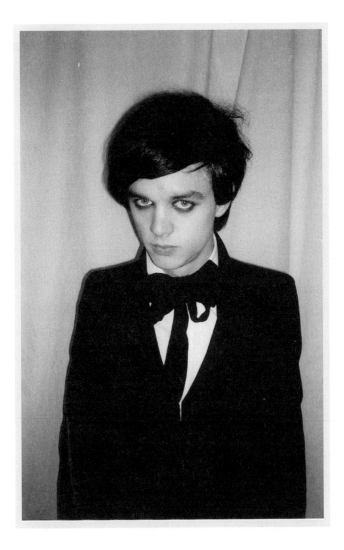

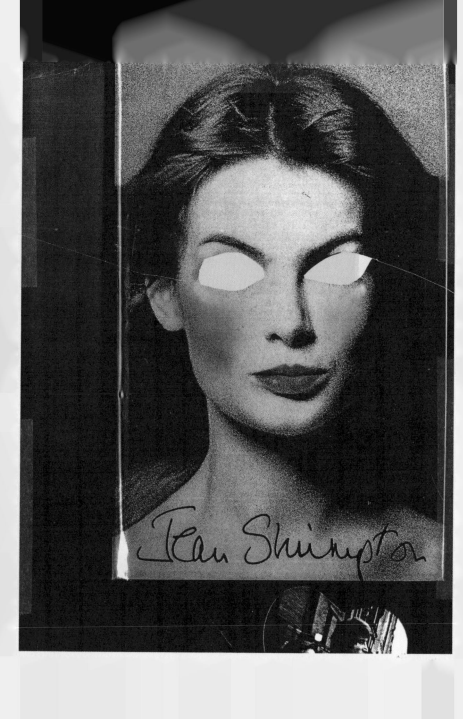

Jean Shrimpton

LOOKING effortless takes a lot of effort.

When I get new Converse I dedicate some time at home to shoving mud on them so they don't look squeaky clean. For some reason nothing makes me feel dorkier than new Converse.

Blow dry your hair with a round brush then at the last minute add a sprinkling of surf spray and water to it and massage the roots to get I-don't-give-a-fuck bed head.

Line the inside of your eyes with black pencil then blink really hard a few times in a row. Clean away the excess liner under the eye but keep enough so it looks as though you've lived in it for a day.

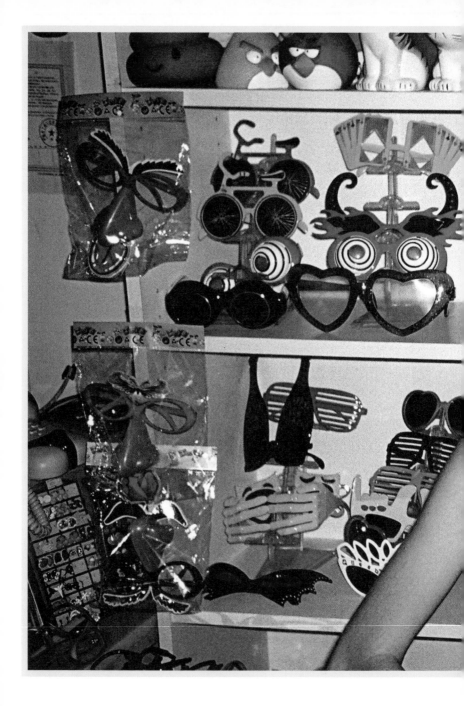

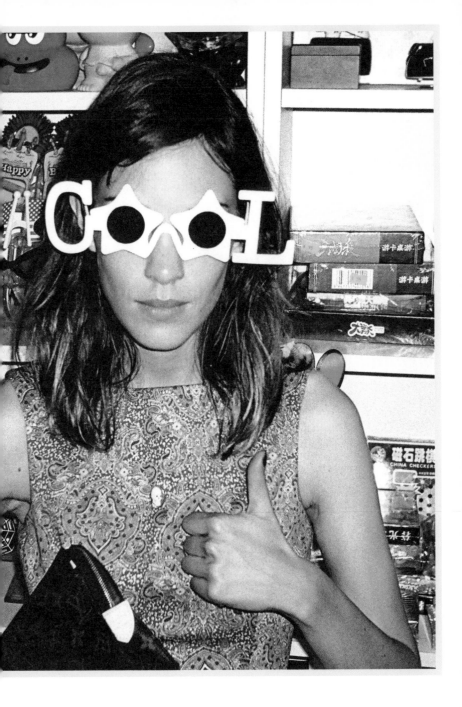

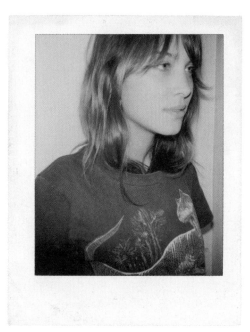

HERE'S a Polaroid of me taken during my modelling days. This photo would've been arranged alongside others on a card and handed out along with my measurements and name (minus the 'Chung' part, so that clients could project whatever nationality they wanted to onto my face). I don't know whether my hair is tucked into my dinosaur t-shirt on purpose or because I've just put the t-shirt back on having been measured and photographed in my underwear by a weary agent. Yes, measured – tits, waist, hips – woe betide any amendments to those numbers during the transition from schoolgirl to woman. (*N.B. you were allowed to increase in height.*)

Rediscovering this picture reminded me that my style evolution was a painstaking process.

Working for commercial companies, shooting catalogue fashion and newspaper supplements, was fantastic in that it allowed me to experiment with items of clothing that definitely do not suit me: combat trousers, shoulder pads, wide-legged trousers, gowns. While other models on castings seemed to adhere to the uniform of skinny jeans, skinny vest, skinny legs, off-shoot I preferred an oversized dinosaur t-shirt and denim miniskirt. Discovering my own personal style came via a long process of elimination, and once I was comfortable with which shapes suited me, I could then experiment within that silhouette. In the early 2000's my bedroom floor was littered with offcuts from various charity shop dresses that I'd hacked apart with some blunt scissors in an attempt to 'rework' the item. I sometimes still do this, and I still like dinosaurs.

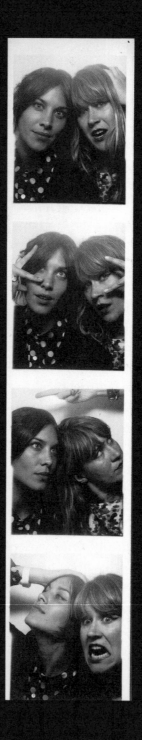

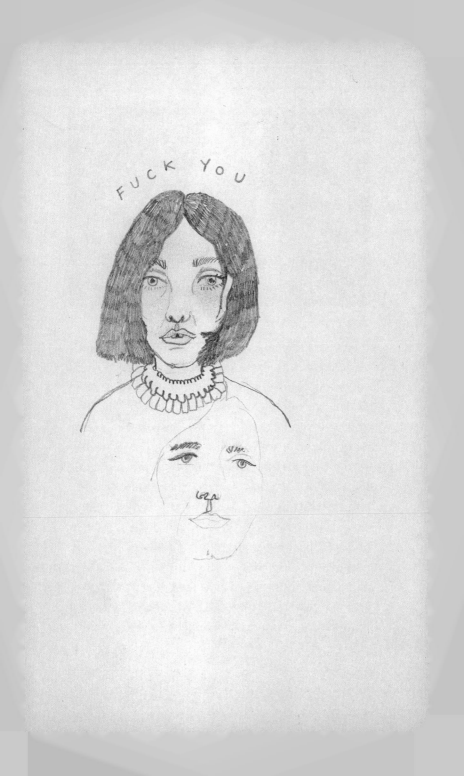

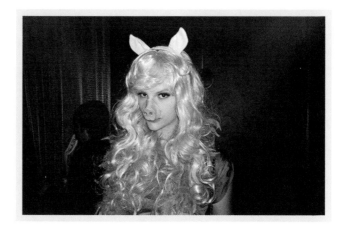

THE night before a hair appointment my hair will decide to look amazing. Without fail. I will get weird and clingy about the length I have patiently waited for and start getting cold feet about a trim. I think my pre-cut anxiety stems from many years of being lied to. I now understand that hairdressers tend to have problems with measurements and so their inch roughly translates as five inches. This is the only explanation I can come up with for how a 'little trim' can and will become a pixie cut. Anyway, once I'm actually at the salon I will suffer the indignity of donning a grey robe with poppers at the neck and wait patiently with the other customers as we read outdated magazines in heavy plastic covers, as if the contents of *Red*, or *People*, is something we should be ashamed of. Trying not to overhear conversations can be tough so often I will listen out for some salacious gossip. Over-sharing is rife in salons because once the chat about where to holiday is over the next hour can morph into a tell-all as if the station you are sat at is a confession booth. I often pile on the make-up on a haircut day because there is nothing quite like the combination of salon spotlights and a towel turban to really play up your worst features.

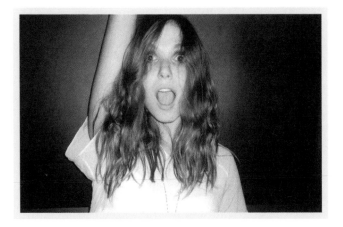

THE bad hair stick has hit us all at one time in our life. Throughout my teenage years I allowed my father to be my hairdresser (hormonal confusion/misdirected optimism/convenience?). It is important to note this is not a profession he had ambitions in, nor was it his idea. I can only presume at some point having observed him battle an unruly hedge with some garden shears I thought it appropriate that he give me a Joan of Arc bowl cut.

Other mistakes have been made. As a model I was frequently subjected to some dramatic dye jobs that made me want to do just that, and then there was the time I wanted to be Kurt Cobain and deliberately added 'grown-out roots' to my shaggy bob. This look is not yet massively embarrassing but I know someday in the not-too-distant future it will make me cringe.

Julie Christie

Mia Farrow

Winona Ryder in *Heathers*

Jane Birkin always

Mick Jagger in the 60's (N.B. *the* not *his*)

Snow White

Child Natalie Portman in *Léon*

PEOPLE WITH BAD HAIR

Everyone in the years 1980–1989

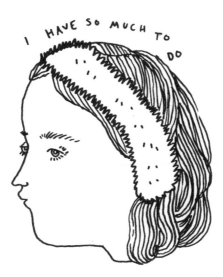

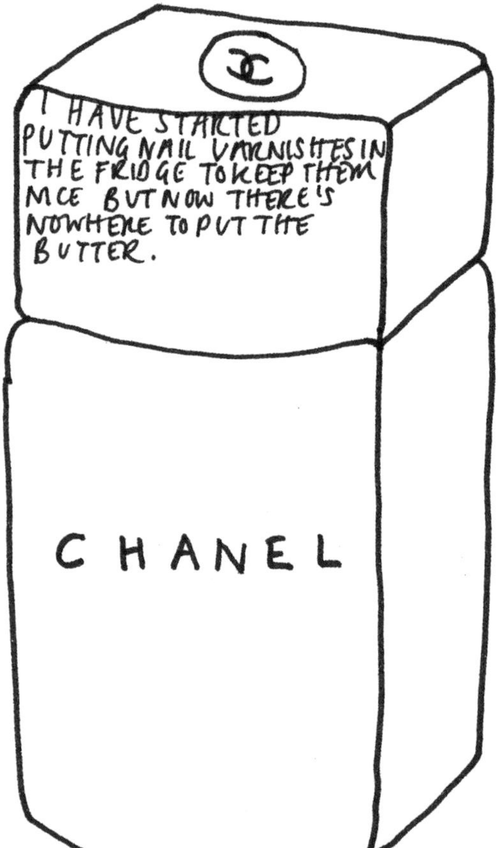
I HAVE STARTED PUTTING NAIL VARNISHES IN THE FRIDGE TO KEEP THEM NICE BUT NOW THERE'S NOWHERE TO PUT THE BUTTER.
CHANEL

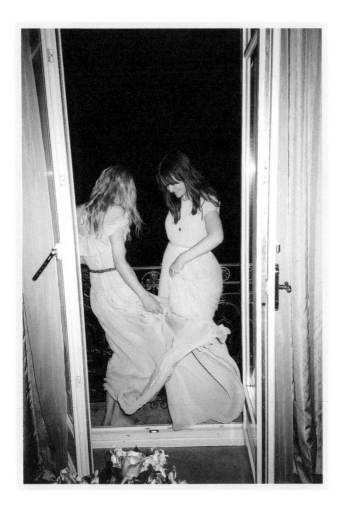

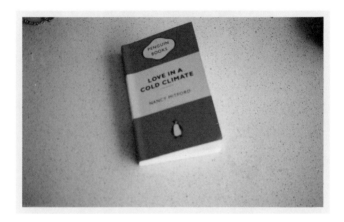

Boys say they don't mind how you get your hair done. But then they leave you for someone with really great standard girl hair and the next thing you know you're alone with a masculine crop crying into your granola.

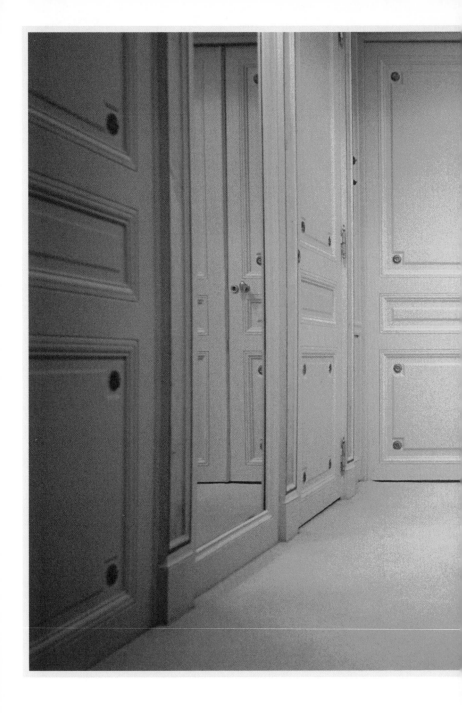

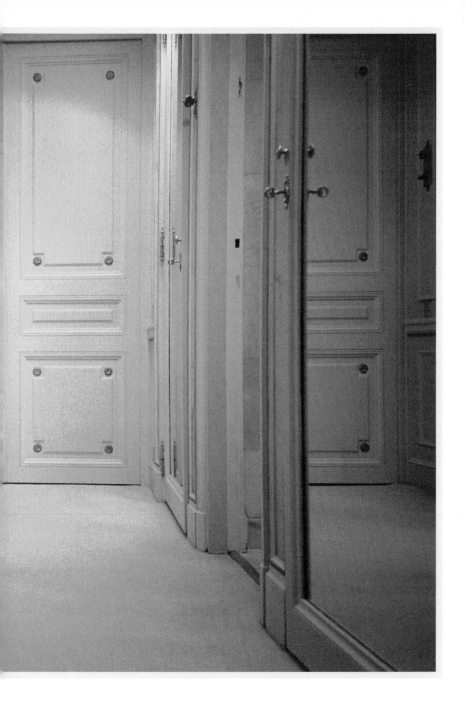

GYM clothes are inherently tricky: you wear them so that you can look good, and yet nobody ever looked good in spandex. I am about as far from being a natural gym bunny (see lack of muscle tone) as an actual bunny, and yet in my few attempts to remain healthy/stave off old age, I have over the years embarked on various forms of exercise. My latest fad is Gyrotonics, a pursuit my best friend has dubbed 'poncy luxury exercise', because when she came to see me do it (weird) she noticed a. it cost a lot to partake, b. to an outsider it looks as though an instructor is moving your lifeless lazy limbs around and c. the day she came to observe, Björk was in my class. Aside from trying to explain what Gyro is, the main thing I have issues with is finding an appropriate outfit to do it in. Initially I was turning up in pyjama bottoms and a bad t-shirt but quickly cottoned on to the fact that going to the gym means you have to leave your house. If you leave your house in PJ's and a ratty t-shirt you should be prepared for people to think you're incredibly lazy and/or having a hard time. In an attempt to sidestep this predicament I have of late adopted proper workout attire. It does not suit me, it does not suit anyone. Why does anything workout-related look eighties?

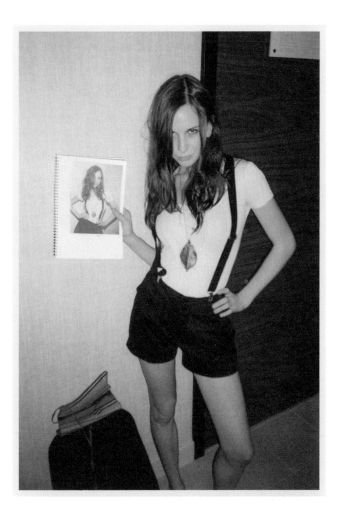

*Don't wear this to the gym even if you have
a photo of you wearing it in a magazine.*

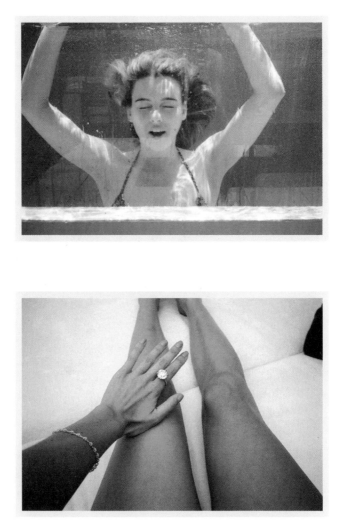

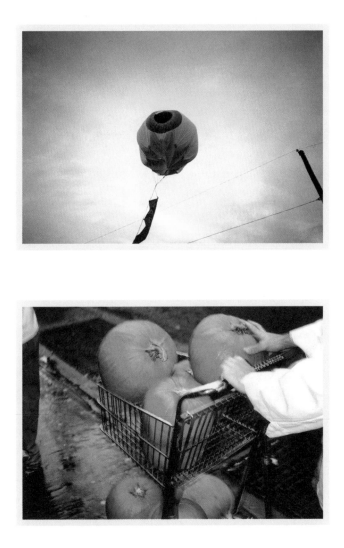

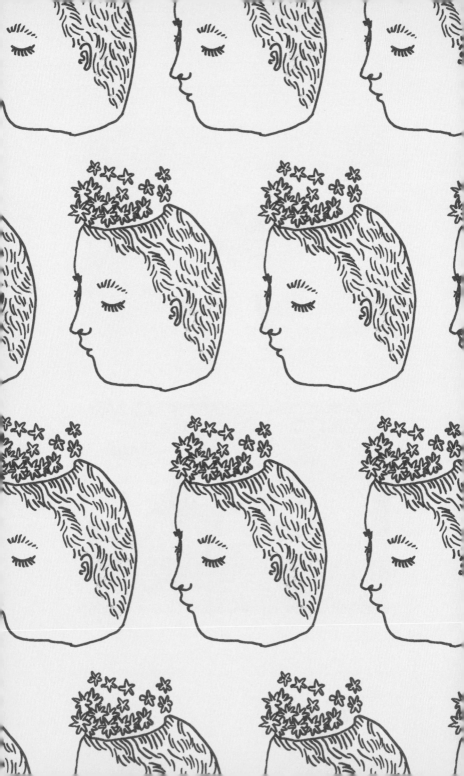

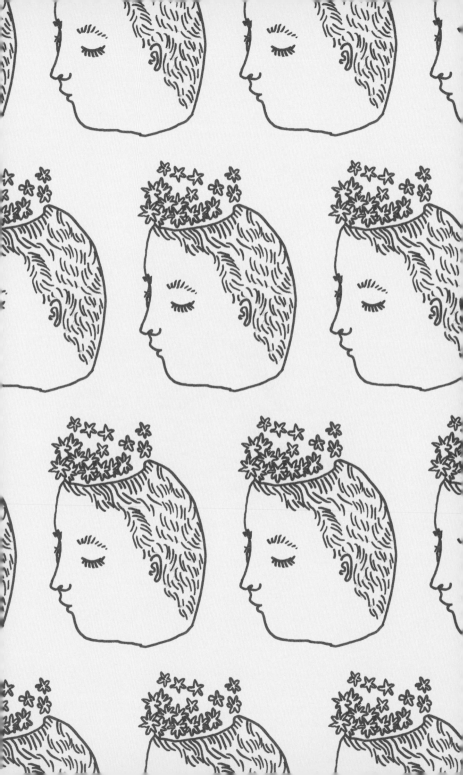

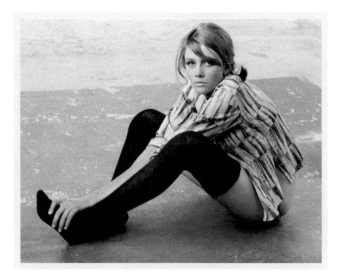

U N D E R W E A R was the last thing I upgraded when my wardrobe began to flourish as I reached my twenties. The Disney-themed knickers were the last to go. They were also probably the last pair of comfortable underwear I will own until I reach my seventies. My first foray into buying more pricey pants left me feeling confused – it transpires that the line between expensive lingerie and the dirt-cheap kinky garments you might find in a sex shop is finer than one would hope. The general rule seems to be the more expensive it is, the less there is to it. Nipple covers and thongs can cost hundreds of pounds – and that's fine apparently. I favour a full brief, and as such look to Charlotte Rampling in *Georgy Girl* and Anna Karina in the striptease scene in *Une Femme Est une Femme* to justify the allure of what could be classed as a granny pant if looked at in the wrong light. I don't believe thongs look okay on anyone, and I'd rather go commando than wedge myself into a g-string.

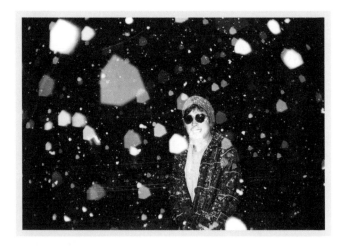

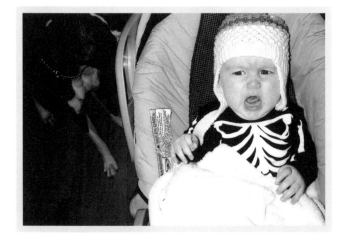

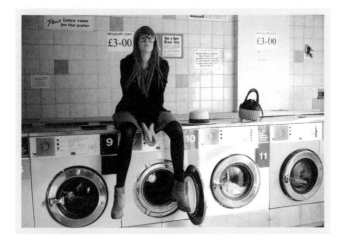

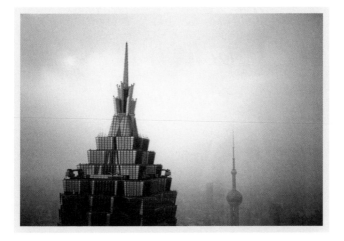

Girl bands
can dominate
music but only
ever one at a time.
That is the rule.
Don't try to
change it.

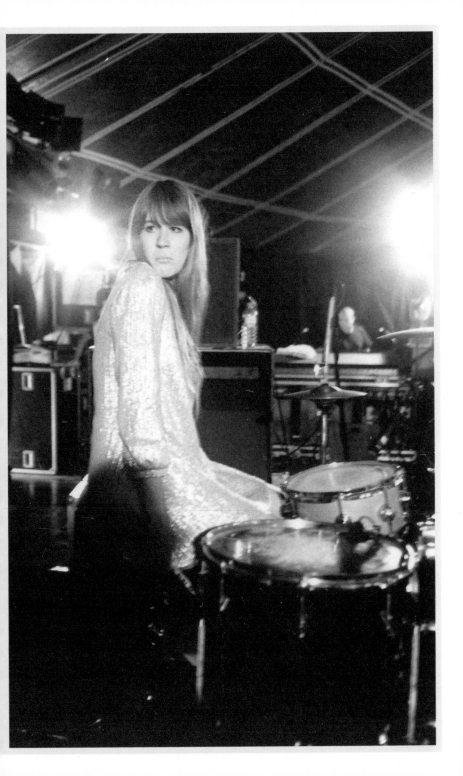

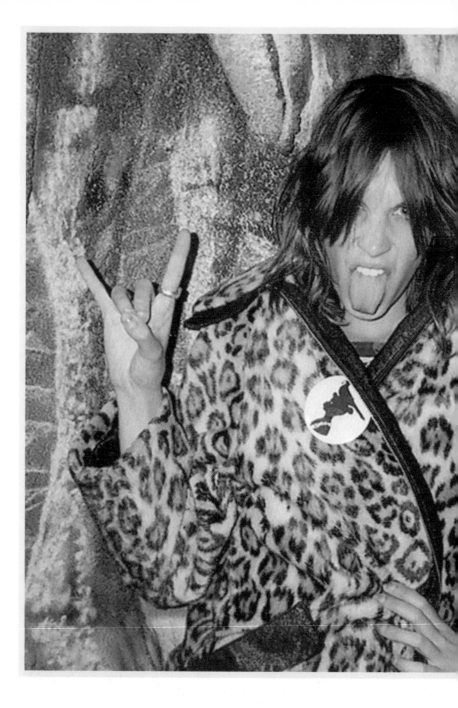

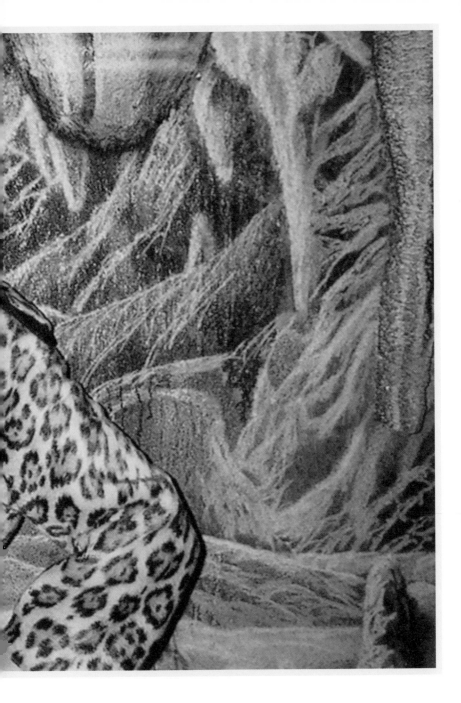

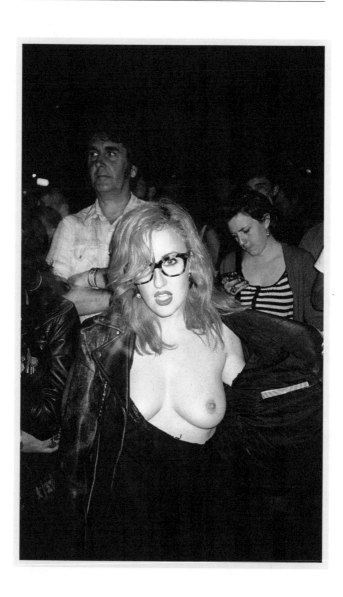

NUDITY is a must at festivals. Along with coming up with clever ways to secretly wee in a crowd, figuring out how to turn your Barbour jacket into a bed and telling the time by looking at the sun. Attempting to explain a British festival to someone who has never been to one is difficult. The mudbath images that are released every summer are something that divide public opinion. I'm fairly certain at some point in my life I will look at an image of a half-naked man caked in mud, grinning and grasping a beer and think 'that does not look like fun', but for the time being I'm happy to look upon that stranger as the posterboy of Good Times.

First and foremost obviously festivals are a place to watch great music. But more than that they are also an endurance test and an experience that can bond you to your pals for the rest of your lives. Festival outfits are something people used to be able to look at objectively and note that the context wasn't conducive to good dressing. Nowadays festival fashion is a genre in its own right and you will be up against stiff competition. Flower crowns seem to be incredibly popular, along with anything sparkly (to be applied to dress or face depending) and of course a wellington boot or two. If you can't find wellies, don't worry, half the people there will be able to show you how to place a plastic bag over whichever stupid shoe you did bring with you in order to stave off trench foot.

THINGS YOU WILL NEED
wet wipes
a blanket
water
glitter

THINGS YOU WON'T NEED
the carrot sticks and humous my mum made me
    take with me to my first ever festival
sleep
a mirror

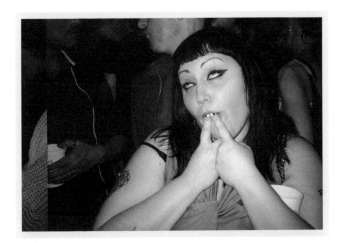

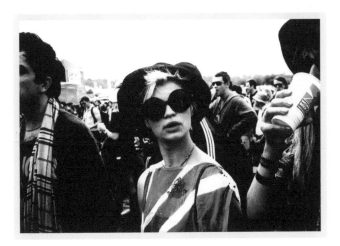

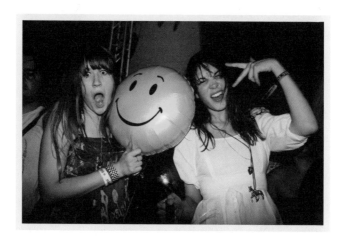

How to rage:
Get a balloon and a best
friend. Go to a festival
in a desert. Be 24.

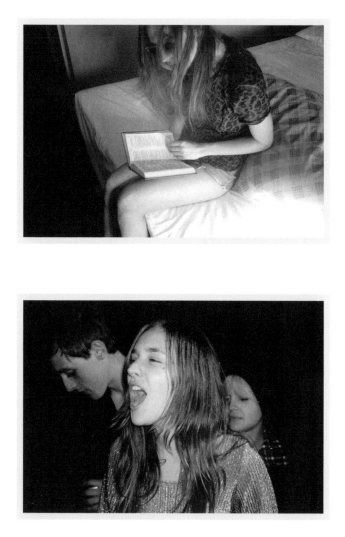

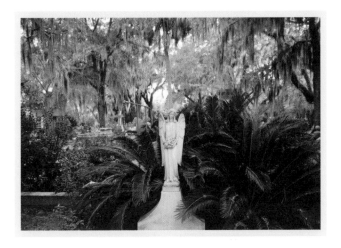

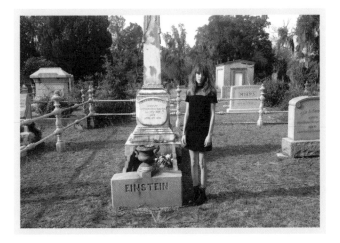

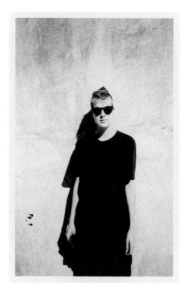

IF tomboyishness is characterized by someone who likes to indulge in boyish behaviour such as climbing trees, getting in scuffles etc then it goes without saying that appropriate attire is required to complete these activities. My favourite outfits are the ones that look easy, or that make you look easy (and not in the slutty sense). I suppose a better word for it is relaxed. Jogging bottoms are relaxed, but that's taking it too far. Tomboy dressing in my opinion is more about an attitude than what you choose to put on. For example, Brigitte Bardot in shorts and a t-shirt could never look tomboyish because I doubt her brothers ever encouraged her to play the part of a rugby ball and threw her around the garden (this happened to me). It also helps that she is not only a megababe but widely considered to be The Ultimate Megababe Of All Time. She could make a litter tray look sexy. But if you were to stumble upon a photo of Anita Pallenberg (during, say, an extensive Google image search) in a skin-tight mini dress she still looks as though she could humiliate Keith Richards in an arm wrestling match. Where some women feel more than comfortable trotting around in skyscraper heels, cinched-in dresses and push-up bras, I sometimes start out in that outfit only to change my mind at the last minute, switch the heels for flat shoes and chuck a jumper over my shoulders. Practicality is high on my list, and limping home to find the plasters when I could be out dancing all night sounds like a shitty way to end an evening. This may explain why I sometimes arrive at a party looking like a crazy cat lady, but that's OK because I don't actually own any cats … yet. I'll always prefer a girl in an oversized t-shirt as opposed to an undersized boob tube but that's because I'm a girl, or a tomboy, and not a boy. I'm confusing myself so I'll end this here.

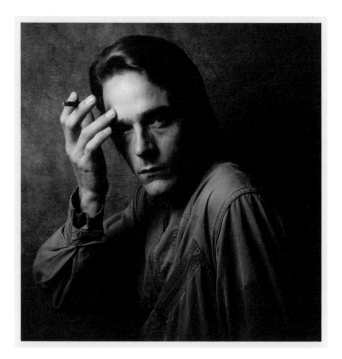

LOOK at Jeremy Irons' floppy hair. Just look at it! You just know that this is a man who will exclusively wear his jumpers over his shoulders, because if he weren't on stage he would definitely be at the country club. I'm not a crazed super fan of Mr Irons and I can see why it might seem odd that he be included in my Style Icons list when so many others have been overlooked. But that doesn't matter. What matters is that Jez is someone I like to use as a human screen on which I project my idea of what he might wear. My version of Irons is preppy and disheveled. All tobacco pockets, monocles and neckerchiefs. I wear stripy shirts and cardigans in his honour. My friend Steph and I are so obsessed with imagining what Irons would do that I have taken to calling her 'Jeremy'. I know.

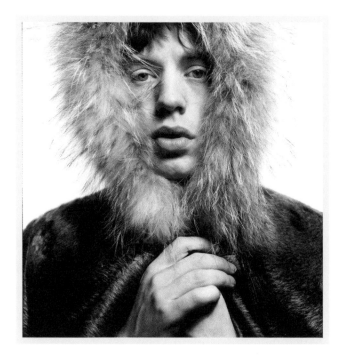

BEFORE he was wearing black trousers, a t-shirt and weird Air Max, Mick Jagger dominated the 1960's and 70's as the embodiment of cool. I like how musicians can put together an outfit that will look good onstage and reflect their persona, and how that then informs what they wear offstage. In 'Sympathy For The Devil', every member of the Rolling Stones look primed for what today would be a fashion shoot, but then was really just their everyday garb. People in the fashion industry constantly reference the 1960's and bands: I think it's because of how free and experimental people were then and how that was reflected in their sartorial choices. Musicians make for interesting style icons because they are so unafraid of experimenting with clothes. Once you've had the confidence to wear say a glitter cape on a stage in front of thousands of people and nobody bats an eyelid I imagine your perception of what's acceptable to wear in daily life changes. (This shot is by David Bailey. I attempt to recreate it every time I wear a hood.)

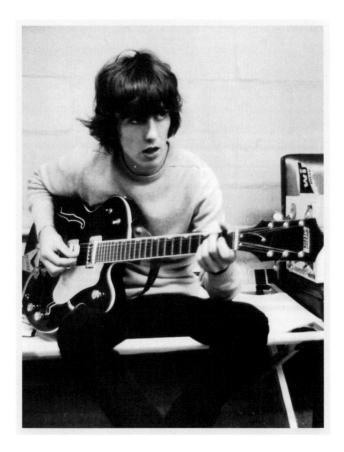

IT'S pointless trying to choose a favourite Beatle because I love them all equally. But, there is something about the way George Harrison wore his clothes that I adore. Often I will turn to men for style ideas and I find Harrison particularly inspiring. Denim on denim has often been cited as a big no no, but on George it works perfectly. His transition from teddy boy to rocker to mod to hippy to perm is fascinating to research. I enjoy the 'pioneer years', which consisted of floppy hats, military jackets and neckerchiefs. Even relaxing on the beach he chose to wear a worn-out baggy t-shirt with a red woolly hat. No trousers, but definitely a hat? It's confusing but fantastic. I must also applaud how, later in life, he managed to make a moustache sexy. That is a really difficult thing to do. Some people are natural-born clothes-horses – George Harrison is one of them.

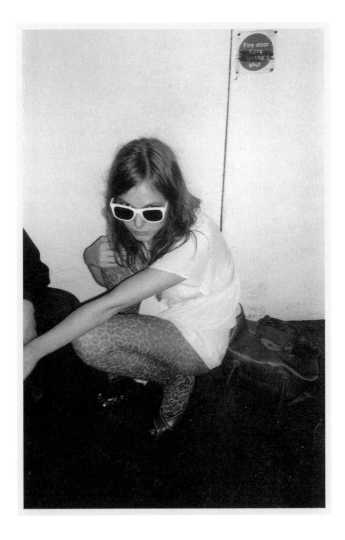

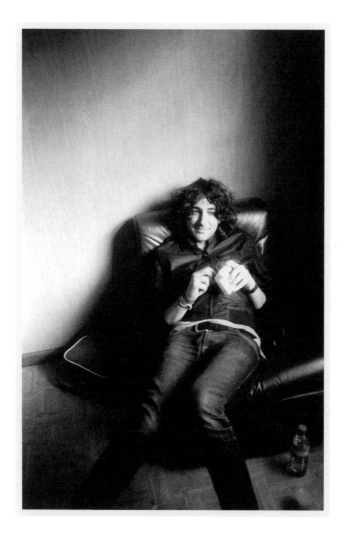

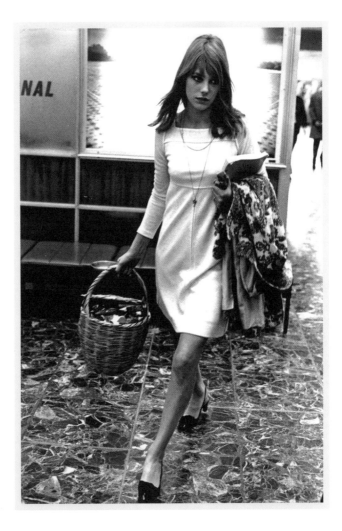

JANE Birkin has influenced me greatly, without really doing much. I mean, she's done loads but it's really her look which I find so inspiring. That gamine figure, the gap-toothed grin, perpetual mega-babe hair ... the list of her attributes is endless. I first saw her rolling on some colorama in just a pair of tights in the 60's film *Blowup*. There are plenty of pretty people on the planet, but the thing I most admire about Birkin (aside from the unaffordable Hermès bag named after her) is her spirit. Her tomboy attitude sets her apart from any of her contemporaries. As well as staring at photos of her for style inspiration (hoping if I look hard enough I'll become her) I have also been to see her perform and she was the most graceful, charming creature ever. At sixty-five she stood on the stage shoeless, in a tuxedo, with her messy hair, and her mastering of the French language. She reminded me that you can dress tough without compromising your femininity. Thank you, Jane Birkin, for providing me with infinite outfit ideas and the confidence to dress like a boy but act like a girl.

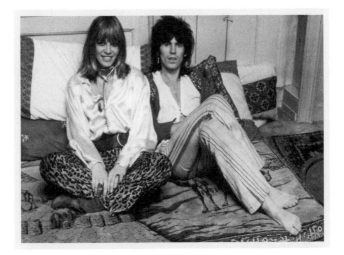

GROUPIE: *a fan of a rock group who usually follows the group around on concert tours.*

Groupie style is all about looking as though you're sexy but low maintenance. If you're going to travel with a rock group you better pack light. I suppose that may explain why groupies look as though they're wearing all their belongings at once (makes it easier to hop on a tour bus at the drop of a fedora). If showers are scarce, hair brushes definitely aren't going to be readily available (see Pamela Des Barres's wild locks). Anita Pallenberg was the queen of short shorts, tiny tees and scarves. Bianca Jagger used to clip her backstage pass to her platform ankle boot. Marianne Faithfull was famed for her natural beauty and ample bosom. Generally, looking as though you could potentially be *in* the band and not just *with* the band is a great way to sneak backstage.

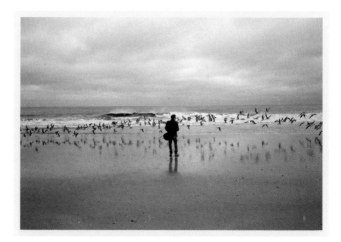

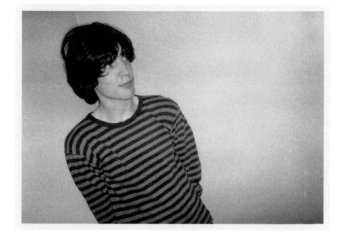

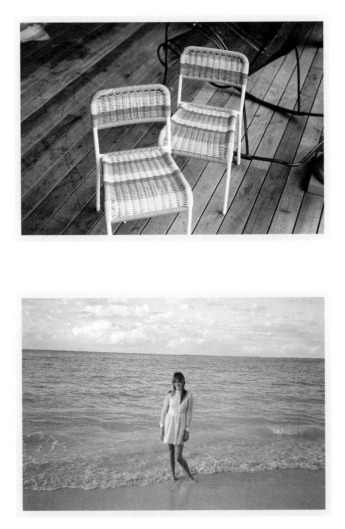

MOST great songs are about break-ups or being bummed out in general. If you want to indulge in a sad fest here are some tunes that will really egg on the blues:

'Waiting 'Round to Die' – Townes Van Zandt
'Blues Run the Game' – Jackson C. Frank
'Strange' – Patsy Cline

Did you just fall in love? Uh oh:

'I Only Have Eyes for You' – The Flamingos
'And I Love Her' – The Beatles
'You Send Me' – Sam Cooke

A G E N D A

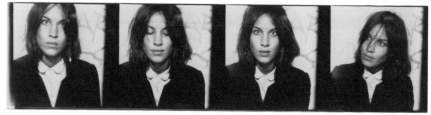

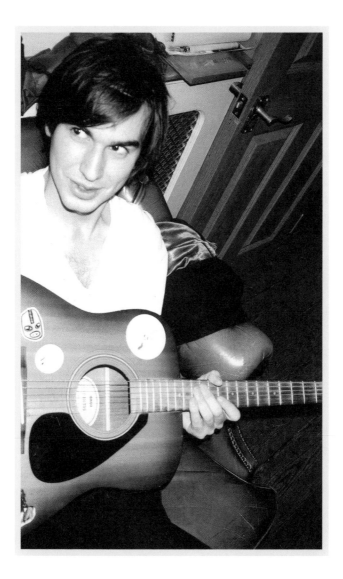

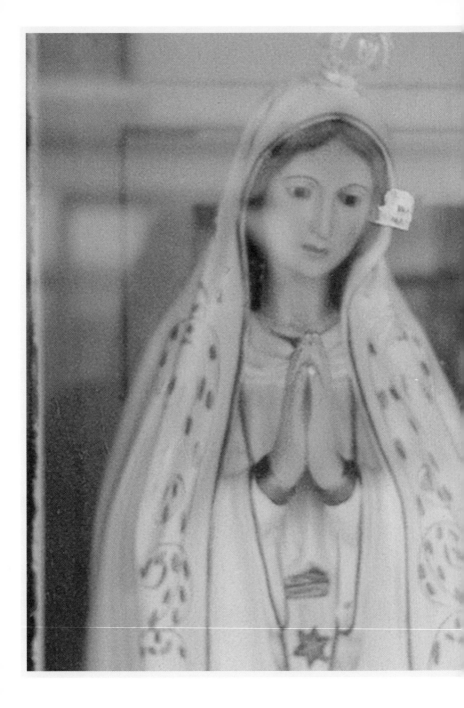

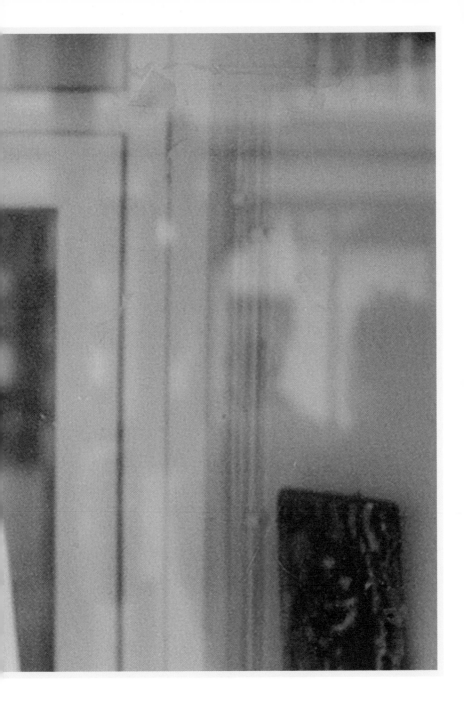

THE problem with heartbreak is that nobody can help you when you're heartbroken. Nobody and nothing. Not the films you watch alone desperately searching for a character who feels the way you do, not the glasses or bottles of whisky you keep by your bed and certainly not Instagram. Instagram will not mend your broken heart, despite your best efforts to post pictures of yourself looking 'happy'. Every time you post a picture of yourself to Instagram looking fake happy a fairy dies. Fact. Also, scrolling through photos of girls your ex may or may not be shagging won't help you. You need to remind yourself that the right filter can be fantastically flattering and she probably doesn't look that good in real life.

Sometimes when I need answers I like to take my questions to Google. I have googled 'how long does heartbreak last?' The result more popular than that was 'how long does heartburn last?' This implies people suffer from heartburn more than they do heartbreak which is a good thing because heartbreak sucks way fucking more than acid reflux ever could. Weirdly though a broken heart does physically hurt. It feels heavy, like someone is sitting on your chest. Sometimes you wake up with pins and needles in your right arm. I met a girl who told me that an acupuncturist told her that if this happens you have a broken heart. The irony of a pin and needle therapist being an expert on needles and pins is fantastic. And that's the other thing it'll do to you. Heartbreak will force you to strike up conversation with anyone who will listen and who might be able to tell you it's going to be okay.

One night in Paris I saw Marianne Faithfull sitting in the corner of a bar. I am a self-confessed groupie – I have never dated a man who was not a lead singer. To me, Marianne Faithfull is the holy grail of Groupiedom. So of course in a drunken haze (it was Fashion Week) I barrelled over to her and just straight up asked her how she got over Mick Jagger. Because how, HOW, do you get over Mick Jagger?!! She said, 'Dahhhling, you can't believe the lyrics.' I don't really know what this means. So I asked my mum instead (about heartbreak, not Mick Jagger (I wish)) and she told me:

'Nobody goes through life without having their heart broken and one day you'll wake up and it will be okay.'

My mother is amazing. She's like a weird oracle. If she wasn't happy living in England baking cakes and listening to the radio she would be in charge of a Witches' Coven. Other things she has said (bear in mind, these were in response to the same situation) include both 'out of sight, out of mind' and 'absence makes the heart grow fonder.' She also said (and this made me do a little puke in my mouth), 'the best way to get over one man is to get under another.' I don't think she intended for me to go on a massive bone rampage but I certainly upheld my end of that bargain several times, so for that gem of information, mother, I thank you from the bottom of my broken heart.

There are upsides to despair. You can wear a blanket instead of a coat and your friends won't judge you. You can smoke indoors because nobody will have the heart to tell an inconsolable girl that a smoking ban has been in place for eight years. And you find out that people are very nice and that they care about you even if the person you care about most doesn't. When somebody makes you laugh when you're sad, that's the most enjoyable laugh you'll ever experience. On a positive day during an outdoor and legal cigarette break I told a friend that I was fine and trotted out the line 'what doesn't kill you make you stronger.' To which she replied, deadpan, 'that's not true, that which doesn't kill you makes you wanna die.'

The nicest thing I heard during the worst time in my life was this: 'you have to suffer heartbreak so you know what to tell your daughter when she has her heart broken.' I'm Alexa Chung and one day I'm going to have a daughter and I'm going to know what to say to her. I'm going to say:

'Nobody goes through life without having their heart broken and one day you'll wake up and it will be okay.'

I can't fucking wait for that day to come.

LEUCHTTURM1917
AGENDA

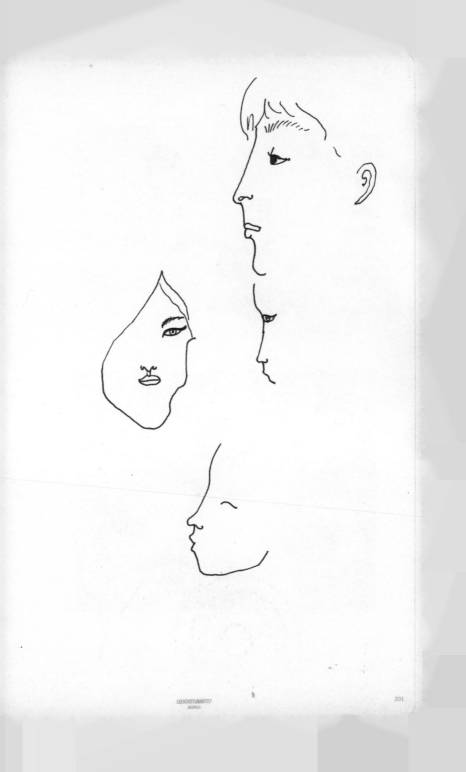

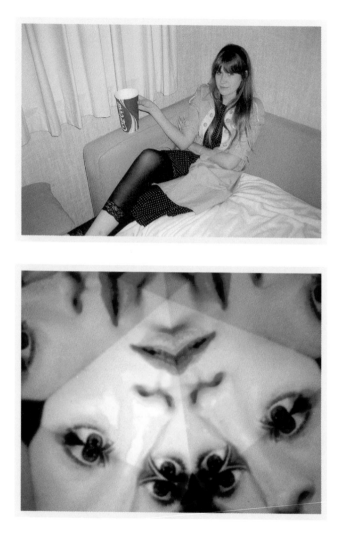

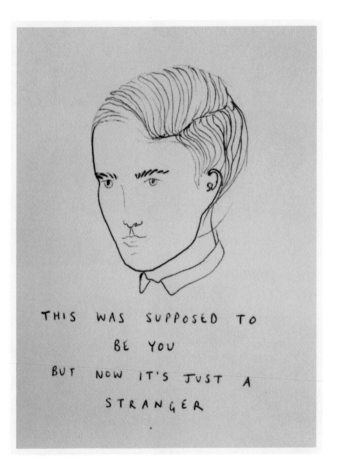

THIS WAS SUPPOSED TO BE YOU
BUT NOW IT'S JUST A STRANGER

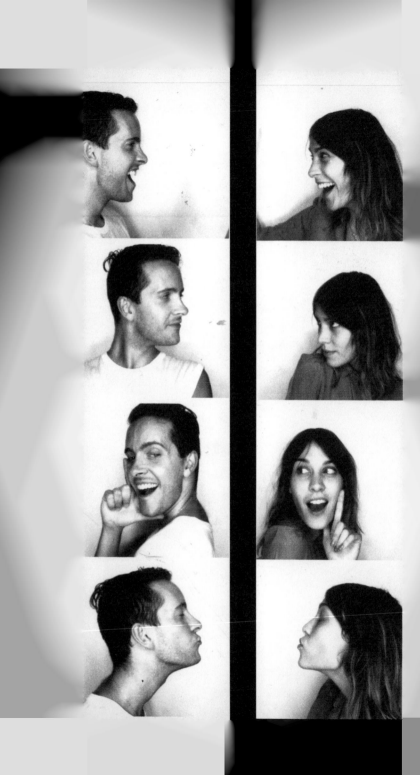

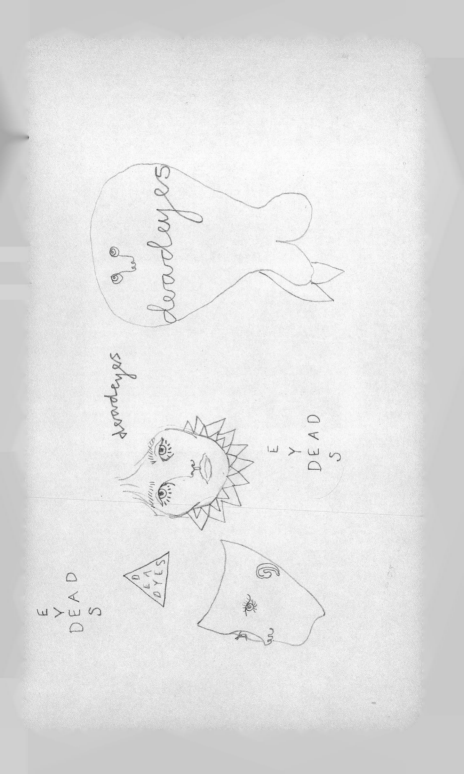

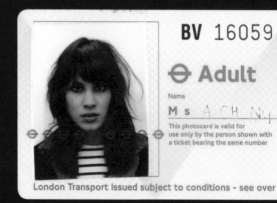

DJing for people is fun until someone comes up with a phone screen that has 'PLAY SOME RIHANNA' written on it. I prefer to play older songs because they're the ones I personally enjoy dancing and singing along to and modern dance music bores my brains out.

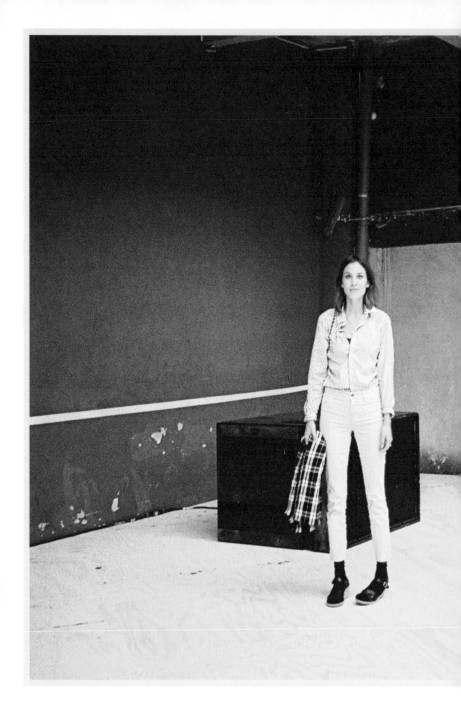

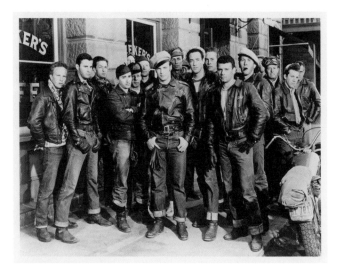

ONE male friend of mine gets depressed in the height of summer and the middle of winter – not because of the extremes of temperature – but rather the effect those temperatures have on his ability to wear his beloved leather jacket. His leather is an extension of his personality, an identity signifier he struggles to live without. Leather jackets, once exclusively the property of bikers and rockers, have in recent years become a staple for any young adult ... which brings me to the downside. There is nothing quite as effective at ageing a human being than a motorcycle jacket. But rules were made to be broken, and I dare anyone to approach Slash, Johnny Marr, or the male population of Camden and Los Angeles for that matter and say 'Sorry lads, time's up'. Long live the leather – it's wipe clean after all.

I myself have an extensive collection of leather jackets, despite the fact that the only way I can tell them apart is by looking at the label sewn into the neck. And yet I will continue to buy them because, like many other items in my wardrobe, they are a perennial classic and I have a weird mental block every time I go shopping that means I forget what I already own the moment I cross the threshold into the store.

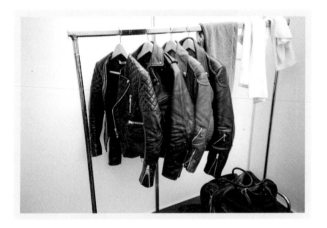

T H E R E are five items in my wardrobe I cannot live without. The cornerstones I rely upon to make newer, weirder clothing look OK. Without them I would be lost.

1. My relationship with my denim hotpants is incredibly special. I pack them in my hand luggage when I travel because I fear that one day we will be separated and I will be forced to go out bottomless forevermore because no other shorts will ever be able to replace them. Since the day I found them lurking in a Brixton charity shop we have become so inseparable that even when I take them off they still retain the shape of my bum as they lie on my bedroom floor. I use them to dress down a flashy top, as a practical alternative to muddy trousers at festivals, and over the years have cut them shorter and shorter so that they are now borderline obscene (they keep getting cheekier). Until the denim disintegrates and falls off me, these particular hotpants are here to stay.

2. A navy blue jumper is potentially the most boring item anyone could design and yet it's my most important possession. The one I own belongs to an ex-boyfriend, and before shops caught on

and made 'boyfriend-fit jeans' and 'boyfriend sweaters' everyone was happily throwing on their actual boyfriend's belongings to keep warm. I have never travelled without it and it has rescued me from many mornings of outfit panic. Once when I was heartbroken a male friend of mine sent me his navy cashmere jumper to wear as a perpetual hug to cheer me up. It worked.

3. My Burberry trench coat is something I saved up for a long time to buy. When I wear it I feel like a French detective from the sixties. Yet I love how quintessentially British it is, in that it's practical yet proper. It was either this or a cagoule. I think I made the right choice.

4. Every woman needs a transportable receptacle to shove her collection of clutter into, and as much as I love some It Bag arm candy I am just as happy to pile everything into a canvas tote. Sometimes I wish I could live like a man and fit everything I need into a single back pocket but that's never going to happen and besides, then I would lose out on the daily drama that occurs when I think I've lost something and have to tip the contents of my bag out only to discover my phone is in my hand. I think a canvas tote bag is

as classic as a Chanel 2.55 and the bonus is you can shove it in a washing machine without having a mental breakdown.

5. I thought I could narrow it down to five items I couldn't live without but I can't, so: ankle boots because you can wear them with literally anything. A pair of Wayfarer sunglasses – wear at night to seem extra aloof. Ballet flats – I can't dance but that doesn't stop me from trying. Dungarees – it's fine that only toddlers and me like these. A white shirt – a no-brainer.

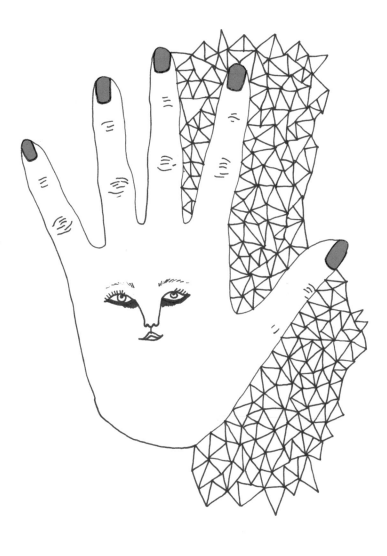

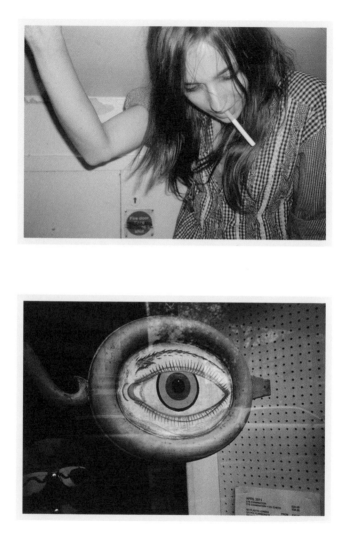

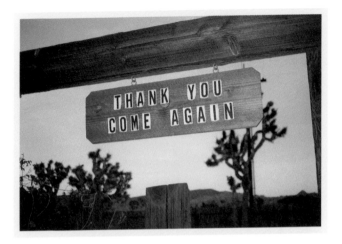

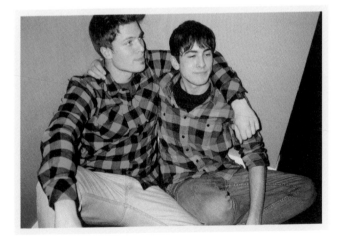

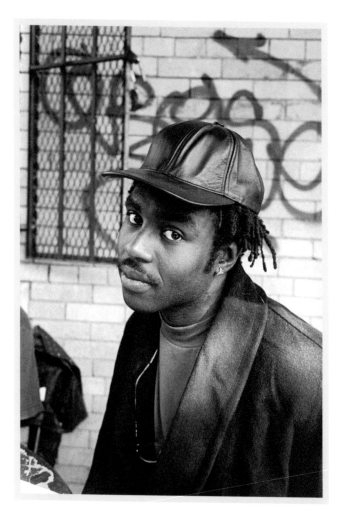

KATE Moss has been voted the greatest hat wearer of all time. They have overlooked Napoleon and royalty, but that's fine. Headgear can be tricky to get right. Christmas cracker crowns are the head furniture that suits everyone so it's a shame you only get to sport them once a year. Veils also seem to look alright on most women, but again the chances of actually getting to wear one more than once can be slim. Aside from crowns and veils, in my opinion the other easiest hats to pull off are beanies and berets. Now beanies do generally look great on everyone, the only problem is they're a bit boyband these days. Also if you have short hair they can be unforgiving. One of the reasons I grew my hair long is because I live in a place which gets swallowed up by winter and it meant that for seven months of the year I looked like a man. Berets aren't just for French people to wear in drawings or for hipsters to wear in East London. Faye Dunaway in *Bonnie and Clyde* makes them look irresistible. So leave your hat on.

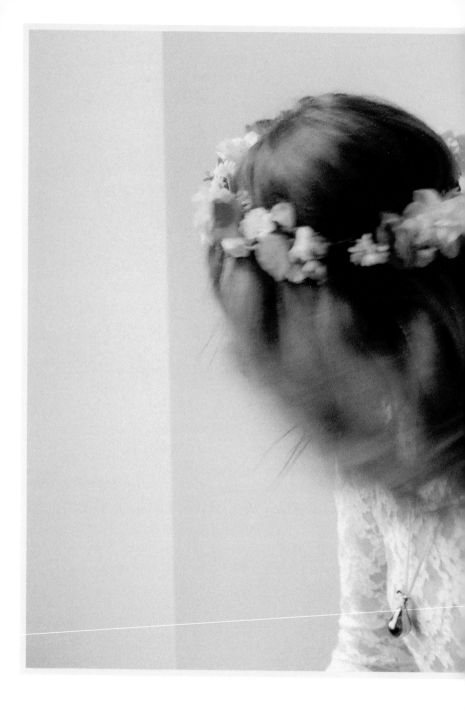

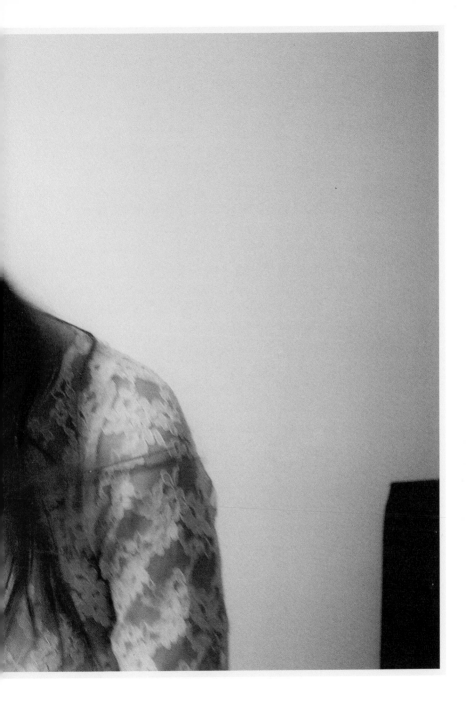

THIS morning I tweeted about spilling coffee onto my lap. This is boring and I blame twitter. Actually Myspace should be held accountable too, for it was there that I first learnt to over-share for the benefit of strangers. Myspace, originally built to celebrate unsigned bands, soon transformed into a breeding ground for the dull. It was there I honed my talent for stalking people. It became a haven for me to express myself via emoticons and songs (my holding page blasted out 'Psycho Killer' by Talking Heads); it was a place I could be boring in technicolour.

Social networking is an ironic name for something that has little to do with connecting us with others and everything to do with self-promotion. It's a one way street, or a one way tweet if you will – 'I'm with so and so', 'I just did this', 'weird question'. Whoever decided tweets should be 140 characters long is a genius. Who knew you could tell a complete story in just three sentences? Now full conversation and convoluted stories seem redundant. Thanks to twitter, Facebook and Myspace, soon I shall resort to grunting, pointing and 'liking' as a means of communication. Now my attention span has been corrupted to such an extent that I often find myself listening to a friend tell me a story I read about on twitter hours earlier and thinking it inappropriate to tell them I already know. Instead I turn to my phone to update my status or 'check in' via a location app. I wouldn't want anyone to miss out on 'where I am' in every sense, would I?

Where will this all end up? Will we completely lose our ability to be private, respectful, subtle? Will romance die? Often I long for a simpler time when break ups weren't made a trillion times worse by photo tagging, and rather than spelling it out for people you could be irritated by something and not feel as though you had to voice your gripe with convenient hashtags such as #dogaccidents, #cake and #snow in case it becomes a trending topic.

The other day a completely shocking thing happened. A man who wanted to ask me out for a drink actually phoned me rather than texting. Actually asked me how I was, actually was bold enough to have a proper conversation with me rather than giving my instagrams the thumbs up as a flirtation device. Whatever next?

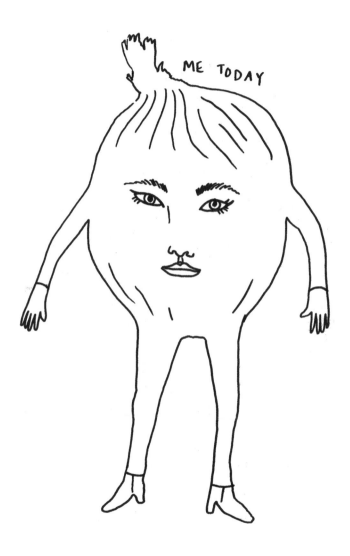

ME TODAY

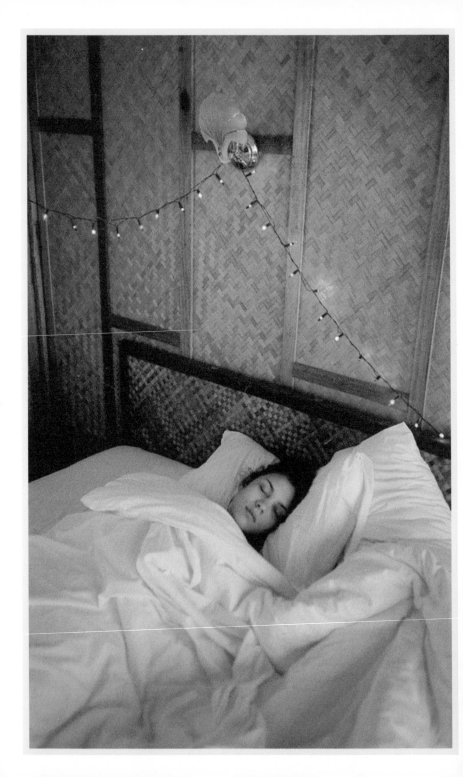

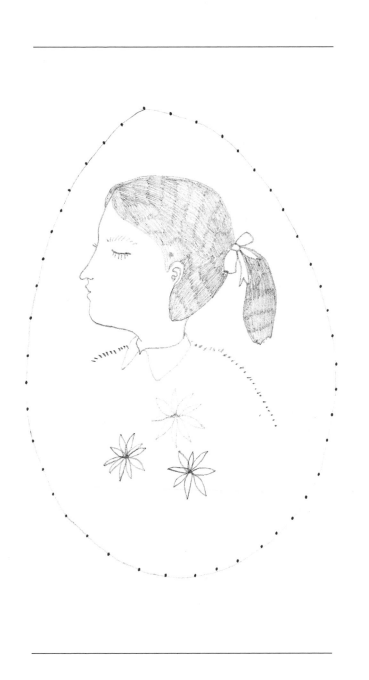

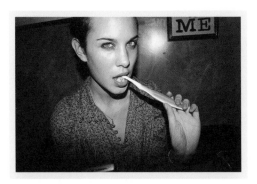

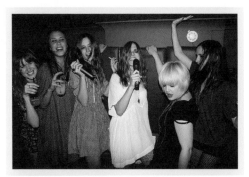

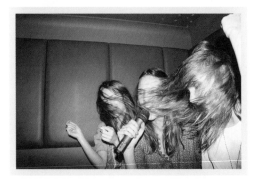

BECOMING a doctor, winning a Nobel Peace prize, making my bed in the morning – these are the things that would make my mother proud. But as you grow older, it becomes increasingly important to take responsibility for your own destiny, and that includes setting yourself goals (no matter how big they are) and trying to achieve them so you can feel good about yourself. I am proud of the fact I've made it onto the wall of my local karaoke joint. This is a huge deal in downtown New York City, an accolade reserved for only the most seasoned karaoke regulars. I'm not quite sure when my passion for screaming Nickelback songs into a soiled microphone began but I show no signs of growing tired of doing it. Sometimes I think if it weren't for my love of karaoke I wouldn't talk in such a husky man voice.

Making it onto The Wall means you know a thing or two about karaoke, so allow me to talk you through some pointers for a great singing session.

1. Set Up: Sound quality does not matter. When in a pinch, if there aren't any bars around that have the requisite equipment for a blinding 'roke session my friends and I have been known to sing

along to YouTube into a mic made of paper.

2. My phone has a file on it marked 'karaoke' – doing your homework is essential. There are good songs and there are bad songs and it is important to know the difference between them. This isn't real life, this is karaoke life. As a general rule I'd say the more cheesy and awful a song is, the better. Nobody wants to hear you doing a perfect rendition of a Frank Sinatra classic. So just bite the bullet and shove on a One Direction tune and all will be well.

3. It doesn't matter if you're shy. I understand very little about not wanting to show off, but thankfully I have friends who would rather crawl under a bus than sing in front of a crowd of people to educate me on the psyche of others. I will say though that the more reluctant you are to sing, the greater the pay off. Once a borderline-mute acquaintance of mine got a standing ovation for singing 'Bump N' Grind'. It was an extremely moving evening.

4. Do not leave until they kick you out. The later it gets, the better it gets.

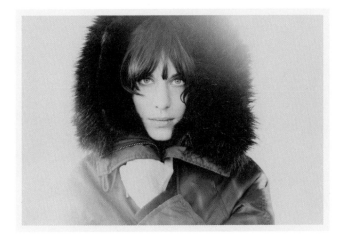

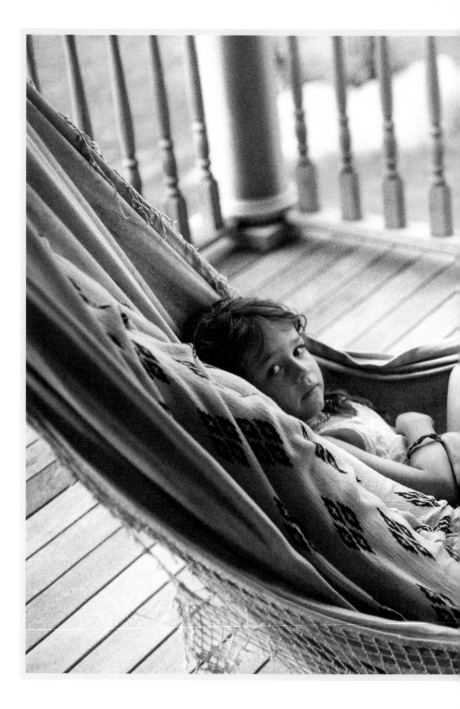

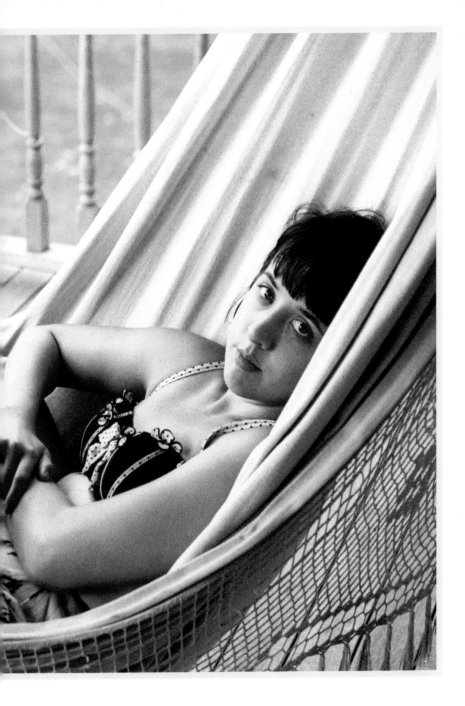

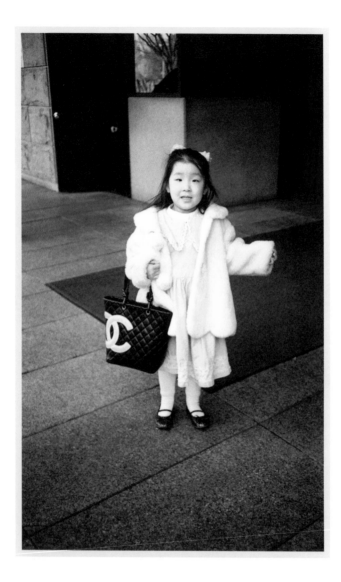

MY friend's daughter, Violet, can put an outfit together like nobody's business. Once I opened her handbag (a red glittery heart affair) to analyse the contents. It contained a photo booth strip of pictures of herself, one dollar and a plastic dog. She has been known to wear a tutu ballerina swimsuit with leopard print coat, Converse and nothing else. A princess dress plus a boy's coat and shoes is her favourite combination. It's a juxtaposition I strongly endorse. If left to their own devices, children dress very similarly to elderly crazy cat women – and I love it. Our affinity for fashion often starts at a young age. Most of the things I wear today are a throwback to items I owned as a child, minus the multi-coloured harem trousers. You know what you like, so follow your gut.

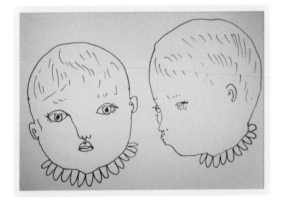

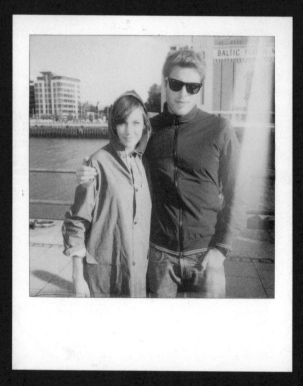

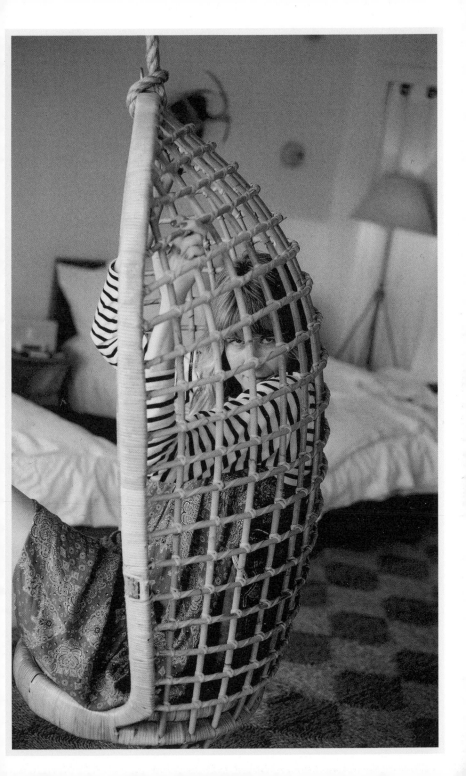

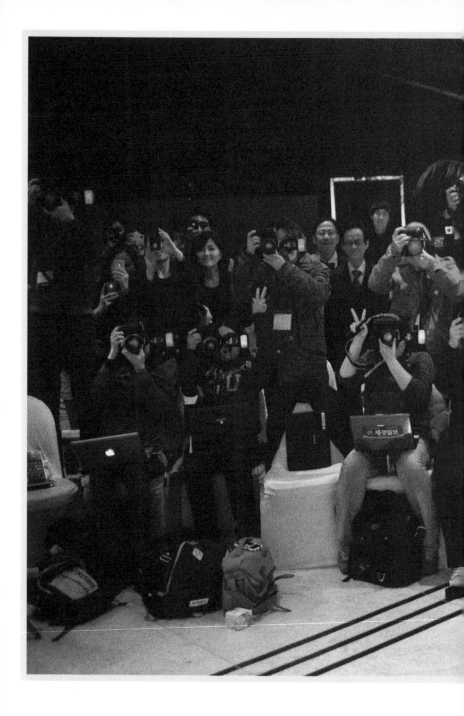

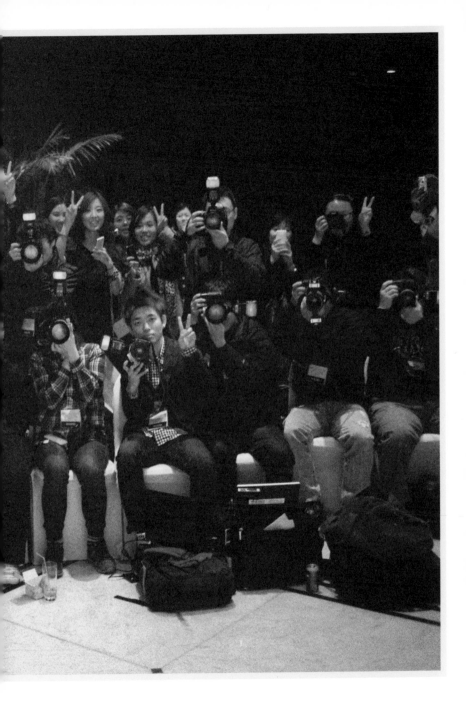

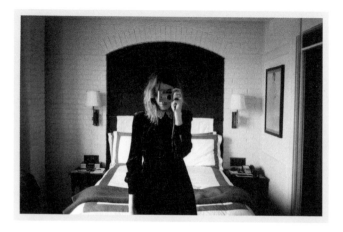

IT'S important in this day and age to master the art of the self-portrait. After all, anyone with an Instagram account knows, this is a vital go-to image once you have run out of cats, babies or dinners to photograph. Allow me (a seasoned professional in the art) to talk you through it. Firstly, make sure the lighting is good. No spot-lighting, no weird harsh daylight, a dimmer switch is your best friend. Next, what outfit do you have on? Have you remembered trousers? Or maybe you're in a dressing gown (that's fine). Anyway, once you're happy with your self-portrait outfit, go and find a mirror. There are two ways to compose this shot: you can either hide your face behind the camera or, if you're having a good day, peek out from behind it – but for God's sake, please don't look directly into the lens. This has to look organic and natural, as if you happened upon a good hair day too fabulous not to capture and assembling the image was as easy as the hairstyle you happened to wake up with. Then snap away. You can keep trying as many times as you like, no one will know (unless they scroll through your photos later in the pub and you've forgotten to delete the rejects). Which leads to the next step: delete the process. You don't want anyone unearthing how long you spent getting this right. Once you're happy with your final image hold onto it, share it and repeat in a few weeks' time.

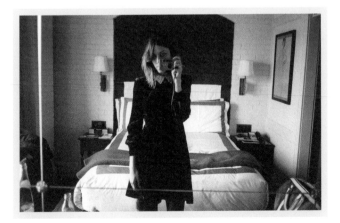

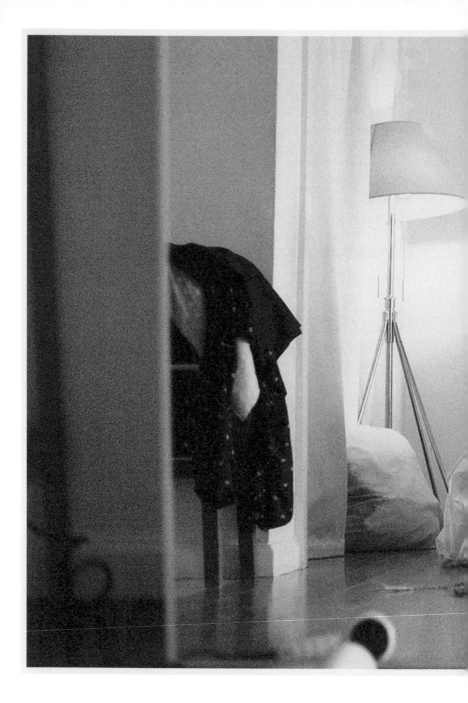

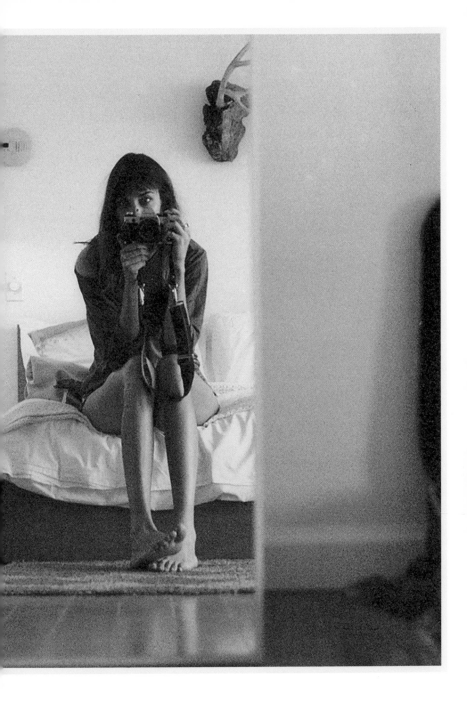

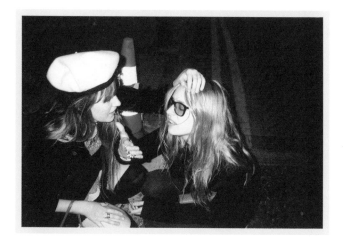

EXITING a car can be tricky, especially if you're wearing a skirt and have been forced to crawl into the far-back-seat of a people carrier. Before getting out of the car you must first master how to get the seat down (nobody likes to see a woman struggle with the mechanics of a flip-down seat for a solid seven minutes, only for the driver to finally come to your rescue by pressing the one button which you had failed to find). Now it's a classic feet-swinging-out-first, a duck of the head and a graceful and swift one-move exit. Give yourself a round of applause if you manage to do this in one movement without hitting your head, flashing your knickers or suddenly remembering you've left your phone in the back.

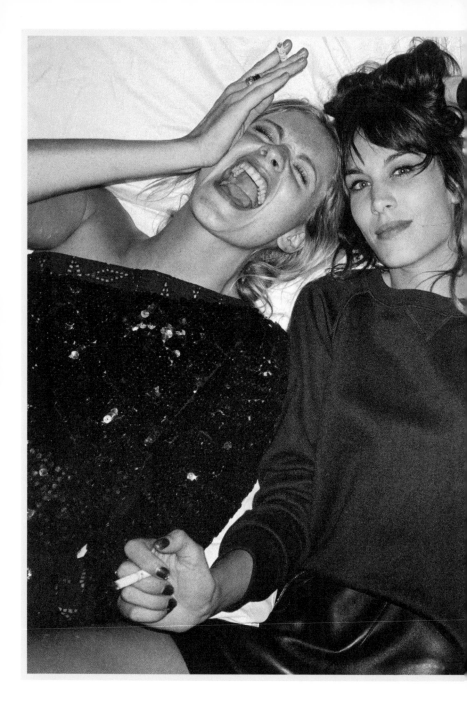

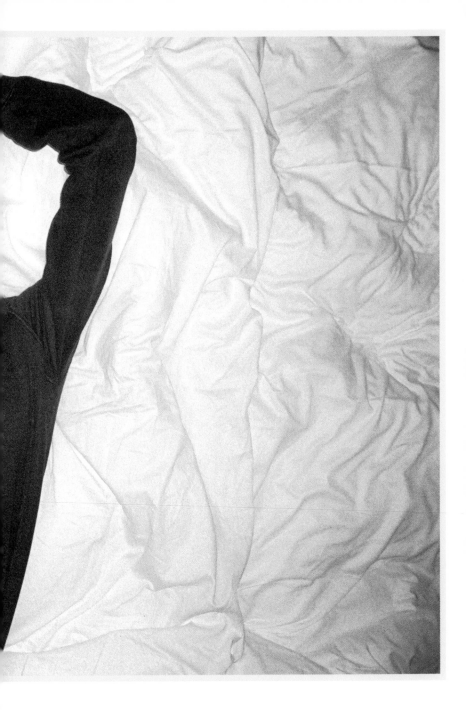

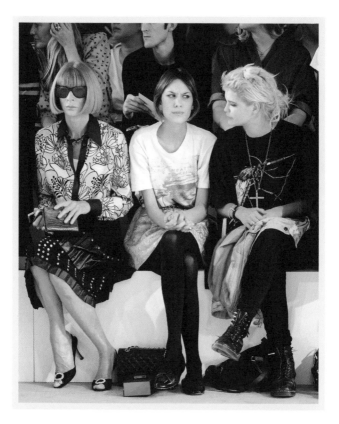

FRONT row politics are convoluted and stressful. On the bench they give you to sit on, each person must only take up one buttock space. This might go some way to explaining why a lot of 'fashion people' are extremely thin (that and the fact sample sizes go up to a size 0, maximum). Once you have found your name it is then essential to scope out who'll be sitting beside you. Quite often I will look down to discover it's someone terrifying. The worst case was when I glanced down to see ANNA WINTOUR and then spent a panicky five minutes prepping for her arrival. (She was actually very nice, I needn't have worried.) A mobile phone with a camera device or an actual real life camera are essential if you want to make sure you steal the best looks walking down the runway ahead of Pixie Geldof or Lily Allen. Sometimes I like to shout 'WOWWW!!' at an outfit to throw the other frowners off the scent whilst sneakily snapping away at the looks I like, prepping to shoot off after the show to the designer to beg to borrow them. Front row small talk is usually based around which parties you attended last night and which parties you plan to avoid later. If it was a big one the night before, water and chewing gum are a must. It is important to never enjoy the moment but rather focus on the fashion show that is happening next so that you don't get shafted in the seat department, arrive late and discover – horror of horrors – there is no room left for you and you will be relegated to the second row, aka the wilderness. If you have a seat, always cross your legs even when the paps at the end of the catwalk shout 'uncross your legs' (it will make you look cool, like you don't care) and try and bring a pair of sunglasses with you plus the carcass of a dead animal, so you fit in. Sometimes the weather can ruin your outfit. If this is the case and rain has soaked you through before your arrival at the Alex Wang show, make like Daisy and Alice and smile through your drowned state.

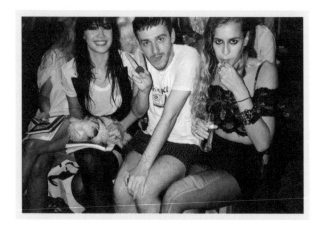

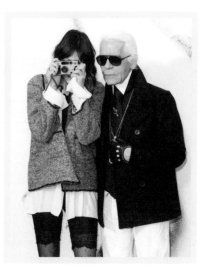

KARL Lagerfeld is very, very funny. His brain
is so expansive it's almost impossible to keep up.
If he weren't the most famous fashion designer on
the planet he'd surely be the most famous something else. After watching a Chanel show you are
often invited to have your photo taken alongside
him. When I'm terrified I try to pretend I'm not
by acting nonchalant. In this photo, intimidat-
ed by a row of photographers and Mr Lagerfeld
himself, I decided to pretend to be busy taking
photos. I think I was also pretending I wasn't
wearing cycling shorts over tights. This particular fashion *faux pas* went unnoticed that day.

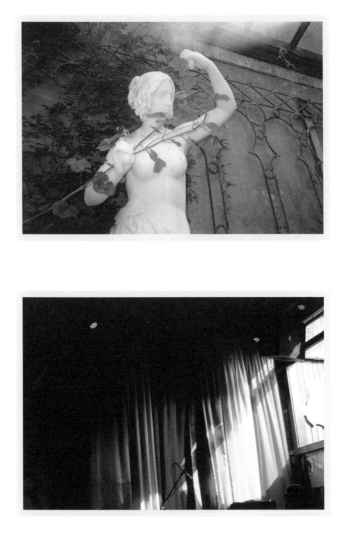

I like to sit in the Rothko room of the Tate Modern because it makes me feel calm and that doesn't happen very often.

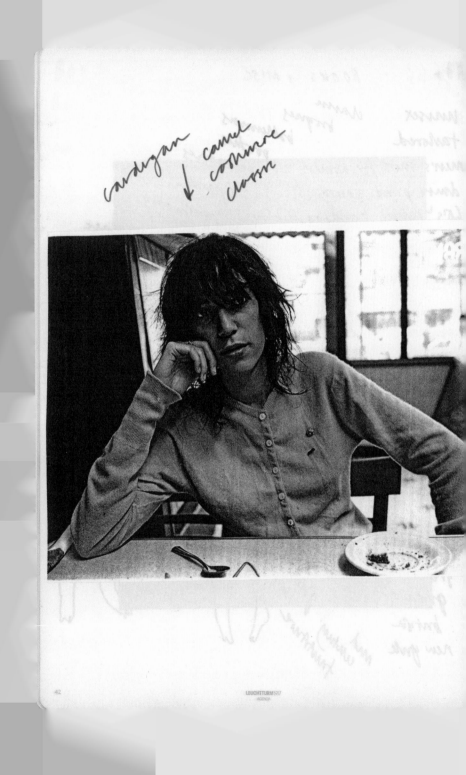

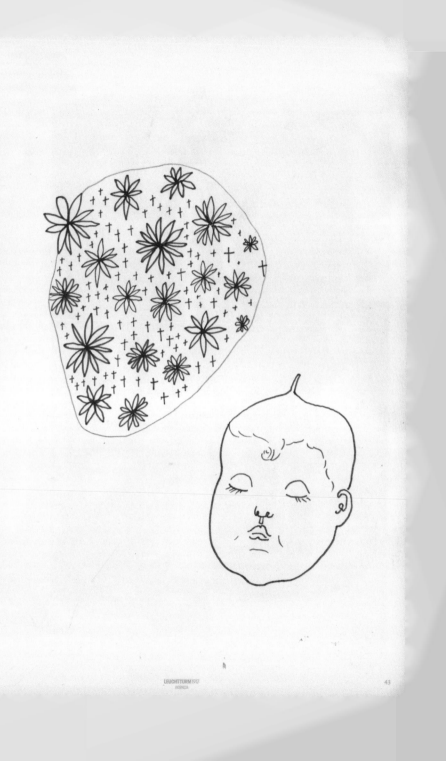

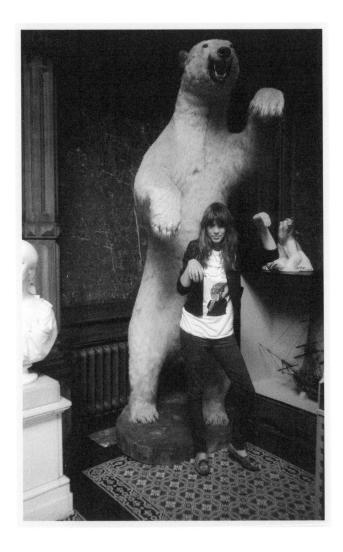

I like dinosaurs like a nine-year-old boy likes dinosaurs. I'm not quite sure why but I just love them. Perhaps it's that they were so huge, or so long ago, or so mysterious. Either way I adore looking at their bones, assembled in the hallways of the Museum of Natural History in New York City. Once I'm done marvelling at the skeleton of T. rex I take a trip to the Water World section (N.B. this is not its official name) which houses a giant whale suspended from the ceiling. Its size is ludicrous, as are the tiny organisms that inhabit the glass boxes at the edges of the room. You can read about all the mental things sea creatures do, like losing fluorescent limbs to evade predators. My goal in life is to become the voice of the Planetarium on the top floor, but Whoopi Goldberg has that gig right now so I have a long way to go.

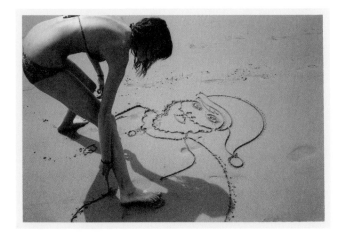

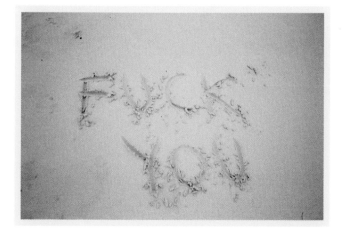

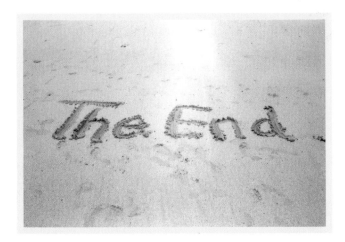